The Everything Beans Book

30 Frugal, Nutrient-Packed Recipes For Every Eater

By Katie Kimball

www.kitchenstewardship.com

Table of Contents

Sides

Pasta

Main Dish Meals

Desserts

Introduction

Whether you're looking to **improve your nutrition or decrease your food budget,** cooking with more beans and legumes is a great way to go. The nutritional value of beans is rarely contested, no matter in what healthy philosophy circles you run.

Before we get too far, let me make sure we all have the same image in your head. I'm not talking green beans, but the legume family: pintos, kidneys, lentils, black beans, etc. The kind of beans that come dry or in cans. Green beans, although a fine vegetable, aren't in the same family as legumes.

We eat a lot of beans in my family, but it wasn't always this way for me. From the time I was a child all the way through to somewhere in college, I really disliked beans. Chili was always on my "don't eat it if you can help it" list, and I avoided refried beans. I'm not sure what happened to my tastebuds – or most likely my texture sensors – but I've grown to love them. The more I learn about beans, the more I find to love.

When I was pregnant with my first child, I focused on eating more beans because of the protein and iron content. After a friend of mine went to a nutritionist for Poly Cystic Ovary Syndrome (PCOS), she learned some information that *really* got me to appreciate beans. Keep reading for the details! You can always find someone who says there's something in almost any food that you shouldn't be eating, but beans have a pretty clean reputation.

The purpose of *The Everything Beans Book* is to take away the mystery or fear that sometimes comes with dry beans. Every recipe has easy-to-follow directions for the most inexperienced cook but also has many adaptations to offer ideas for those comfortable in the kitchen.

Important Recipe Notes (Promise You'll Read These!)

In case you're about to skip reading any more informative text and move on to the recipes, **slow down and read this section!**

These short tips and explanations will help you understand how to make beans work for you in the kitchen, how you can save time on certain ingredients and procedures, and some additional insight into my philosophy on cooking to help you dive into the recipes with more confidence.

- **DO cook large batches of beans and freeze extras** rather than just soaking the amount for one recipe – this saves LOTS of time and energy, both yours and your stove's, as well as dishes. More tips under "Storing Cooked Beans" on page 18.

- **DO make homemade chicken stock** to use in some of the soups in this book – here are the basics:

- Combine chicken bones, with or without meat on them, cooked or raw, in a large pot with cold water and a splash of white or apple cider vinegar. Allow to sit 30-60 minutes.

- Bring to a boil and skim off the foamy junk. Cook on low for 4-24 hours, adding carrots, celery, onions and garlic for the last hour or two and parsley for the final 10 minutes.

- DO check out the much more detailed directions here: http://www.kitchenstewardship.com/MakeStock

- **DO prepare vegetable broth** from time to time when you cook up a batch of beans. Instructions are under "Making Vegetable Broth" on page 18. You can use this in place of water in many recipes or as the base for some meatless soups to remain completely meat-free (we do this on Fridays in Lent).

- **DO keep cooked, shredded chicken in the freezer**. I hate seeing recipes that make me cook the meat first, then proceed with a million other steps. You can even add a frozen bag of shredded chicken into soup if you've forgotten to thaw.

  - For recipes that call for cooked and shredded chicken, make it easy on yourself. When you make that chicken stock, just save the chicken (either pick it off the bones after roasting for more flavor or after boiling for stock for a falling-apart-tenderness) and freeze in 2-cup portions.

  - If you only use chicken breasts, just bake extra next time you're making a meal and run them through the food processor briefly to shred (or hack away with a fork and knife). Measure out 2-cup portions for easy meals later.

- **DO plan ahead by making a double batch of a recipe, then freeze the extras.** This is fail proof for all soups and many other favorite recipes. Once you know you like a meal, it's great to stock up your freezer for busy nights. Each recipe in this book will note if it freezes well or not.

- **DON'T be afraid to make substitutions.** Even for rather novice cooks, recipes where a bunch of stuff goes into one pot are great places to "fiddle" with the ingredients. You can often get away with switching the kind of beans, for example: any white bean usually acts enough like another, in chili you might use black and kidney beans instead of kidney and pinto, some recipes allow for many choices of beans. Having some on hand frozen can make for an easy, versatile meal!

  In many soups and casseroles, adding or deleting a vegetable never hurts. I often toss in a handful of fresh spinach if I'm working through a bag, and using a variety of peppers is an easy way to use what you have on hand. See http://www.kitchenstewardship.com/FreezerPrep for my tips on keeping cut vegetables frozen and easy to grab for quicker meal prep.

- **DON'T overdo your garlic**: Research shows that the health benefits in fresh garlic are released when crushed (which is even better than mincing, so buy a garlic press if you don't have one. You can also chop with a knife if need be.). If you can crush your garlic clove and then wait 7 minutes before cooking, the benefits are increased, and again at 14 and 21 minutes. I generally try to press my garlic first, then saute my onions and chop other vegetables, adding the garlic during the last minute or two of the onion saute. Garlic burns easily and is sensitive to heat, so this is the healthiest way to harness a very healthy food. If you just can't do it or don't have time for fresh, ¼ tsp. garlic powder can substitute for any clove of garlic called for in a recipe. These recipes usually have their garlic doubled, at least, already, so be cautious if you're a person who typically adds extra garlic. Know that it's already been done to a certain extent!

- **DON'T underestimate the spices**: Our family likes spicy foods, so it's possible that I have been heavy-handed with cumin, chili powder, and jalapenos in this book. Always feel free to shoot low on spices, since adding more is much easier than taking some out. Whenever possible, I'll remind you that jalapenos are optional, the seeds make it hotter, and I'll offer a range of measurements for spicy seasonings.

When I cook, my goals are always three-fold: nourish my family, make it taste great, and keep prep and clean-up as simple as possible, with the understanding that using real food is always more work than opening cans and boxes and dumping their contents together. It is my hope that you can find many, many new favorite family recipes in this book and streamline your kitchen time so that you can spend more time with your family, who are happy people because their bellies and palates are both satisfied.

Features of the Text

The Everything Beans Book is set up to be as user-friendly as possible. You'll notice each recipe has helpful icons to assist you in categorizing recipes based on how long it will take to make, if it's kid-friendly or not so much, and if it's a super budget meal or just a less expensive meal with beans.

Since cooking with dry beans always requires an overnight soak, there's no getting around planning for these recipes, and I could say that every one takes 24 hours to accomplish. However, some recipes take a lot of chopping vegetables, while others are more of a “throw together” meal once you've done some simple preparation, even on other days (like having cooked brown rice or shredded chicken from another meal available).

Work Intensity

The Work Intensity icons have one, two, or three clocks, describing recipes that are:

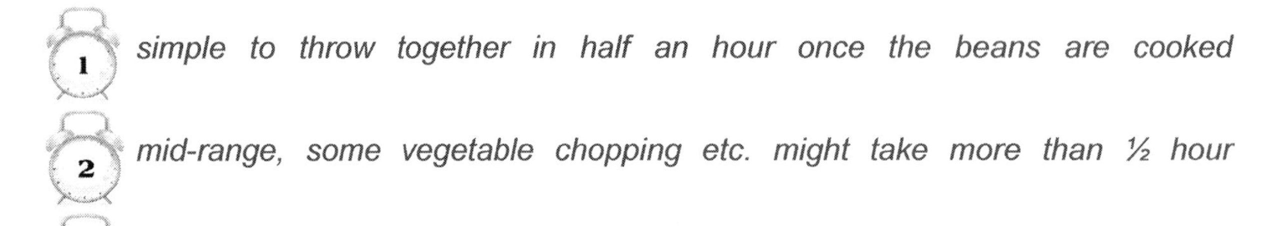

simple to throw together in half an hour once the beans are cooked

mid-range, some vegetable chopping etc. might take more than ½ hour

more complicated recipes with lots of steps or appliances and pots to dirty

Kid-Friendly

An important caveat on this icon is that my kids like nearly everything, and they've been used to beans as a centerpiece of many a meal since they were born. However, I tried to compile recipe reviewers' comments about kid-friendliness plus common sense to apply the following icons:

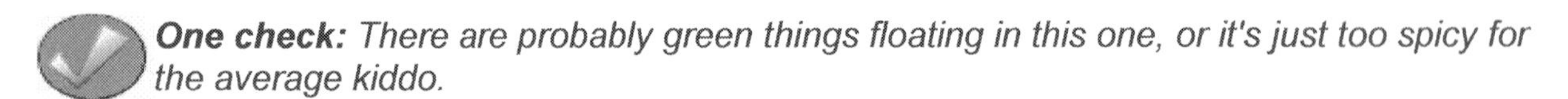

***One check:** There are probably green things floating in this one, or it's just too spicy for the average kiddo.*

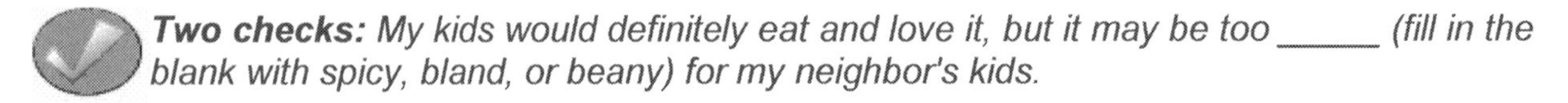

***Two checks:** My kids would definitely eat and love it, but it may be too _____ (fill in the blank with spicy, bland, or beany) for my neighbor's kids.*

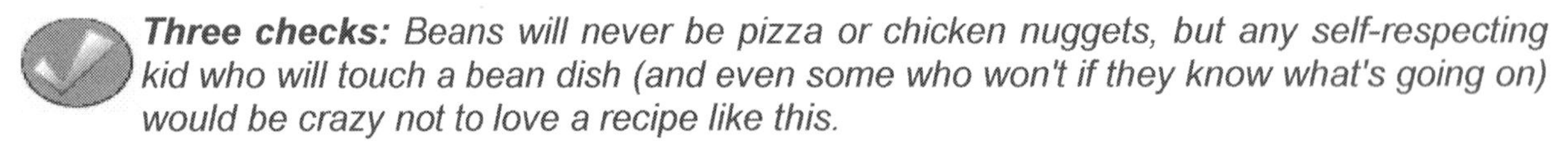

***Three checks:** Beans will never be pizza or chicken nuggets, but any self-respecting kid who will touch a bean dish (and even some who won't if they know what's going on) would be crazy not to love a recipe like this.*

Cost

Using dried beans is simply a frugal thing to do, but some meals are even easier on the budget than others:

***One dollar sign**: An inexpensive meal by any standards, usually well under $5 for the whole recipe, sometimes even the whole meal, side dishes included.*

***Two dollar signs**: A mid-range recipe, one that you could easily make for an everyday meal, and less expensive than a meat-centric dinner like roast chicken or hamburgers.*

***Three dollar signs:** A pricier meal than most bean recipes, either because of some expensive ingredients or the sheer volume created. In almost all cases, even the most expensive recipes in this book are still less than your average meat-based meal that doesn't include beans or legumes.*

Special Diet Notes

- **Gluten-free readers:** Although this book is not gluten-free entirely, many of the recipes naturally do not include wheat or barley. When they do, it's often rather simple to replace barley with rice, wheat tortillas with corn, and use gluten-free pasta. Whenever I had the chance to test it, I tried to use arrowroot starch instead of wheat flour as a thickener (in just a couple recipes). I'll let you know in each recipe if it worked or not. GF recipes are marked GF

- **Dairy-free:** All recipes are flexible for changing out the fats for sauteing and deleting cheese on top, especially if you have a dairy sensitivity. I tried to include all choices for fats and oils in every recipe, but if they're not listed, any of the following fats should be just fine for a vegetable saute in any recipe in this book:

    - Refined or unrefined coconut oil
    - Butter (over lower heat so it doesn't burn)
    - Extra virgin olive oil (lower heat so it doesn't smoke)
    - Well-sourced lard (non-hydrogenated)
    - Beef tallow
    - Palm shortening

    You'll find automatically dairy-free recipes marked CF

- **Kosher**? Although a few recipes call for sausage, they also reference my homemade sausage recipe with which you can use any meat, from ground beef to turkey, to achieve the same results. Any recipe that requires bacon is usually still okay just by skipping it, or feel free to use turkey bacon.

Why Beans?

Two reasons: Beans are frugal, and beans are healthy. (If you're lucky, you'll add "they taste great!" to that list too.)

In our family, we eat beans at least once a week, often as part of a meatless meal but sometimes paired with meat in the main dish or on the side. Most of our favorite soups incorporate beans or legumes. Using beans, especially dry beans, allows me to provide a hearty meal with less meat or no meat, thus freeing up funds for me to purchase the meat, eggs and milk I want to feed my family and keep the budget in the black.

Although I'm a firm believer in the health benefits of meat, I'm also a realist. Meat and dairy products are by far the most expensive items in a food budget, and if you want to devote funds to high quality, well-raised meats, most of us average families are going to have to find a place to cut back elsewhere.

Beans are Healthy

Beans will give you the following nutritional benefits:

- Protein (1/2 cup = 7-8 g, 15% RDA)
- Fiber (best if long soaked and long cooked)
- Iron (1/5 RDA, eat with Vitamin C to increase absorption)
- Folic acid (HALF recommended daily amount in ½ cup)
- Zinc
- Magnesium, copper, vitamins B1 and B6
- Antioxidants
- Omega-3 and omega-6 fatty acids

All those nutrients can improve your health by:

- Lowering LDL (bad) cholesterol
- Reducing risk of heart disease
- Improving digestion/reduce constipation
- Having a low glycemic index = good for diabetics
- Filling you up longer = good for dieters
- Reducing risk of cancer
- Providing folic acid, which is especially important in pregnancy for healthy babies!

Sources: http://bit.ly/1ne6WIS, http://bit.ly/1ixK0xc, http://bit.ly/N9Zttw, http://bit.ly/1eYM2Tr

This is a serious list. If you are pregnant or might become so, diabetic or pre-diabetic, have a family history of heart disease or high LDL cholesterol, want to lose weight, have digestive issues, or are just on a budget and want healthy food…EAT MORE BEANS!

Beans, Beans, All the Time

Are you curious about the info from my friend's nutritionist that *really* convinced me to include beans more often? First, I'll tell you that the diet my friend was put on was pretty strict: no sugar or carbs of any kind, no caffeine, 7 servings of veggies, 5 of protein every day…and beans 3 times a day, once at each meal. Three times a day! That's beans and eggs for breakfast, beans on a salad at lunch, beans in SOMEthing at dinner…every day. Phew. That's a lot of beans.

The nutritionist explained that my friend's body was stressed, and that's why she wasn't ovulating. Her analogy [my paraphrase]: *If your mother was sick with cancer, what would you do? You would drop everything and help take care of her. Even though she's the one who's sick, you'd have a lot of stress. It's the same thing in the body – if adrenal and pituitary glands are stressed and over-producing, your ovaries "drop everything" and don't ovulate while your body focuses on the "sick" glands. You must get your body to stop freaking out.*

My friend needed to put her system into complete rest mode: no sugar, no carbs without protein, no caffeine, because all those things make the body work harder and stimulate the adrenal glands.

There are a lot of impurities that our bodies encounter every day that stress out our system. The job of the liver is to clean impurities out of the blood. The bile in the liver, however, can only take so much. Beans will do the job to maintain it and clean out the bile so it's not saturated with "junk". The beans take the impurities out of the bile in your liver and carry them out of your body. Think of beans as the janitorial crew, worthy of a "Dirty Jobs" episode to be sure.

That's why the nutritionist starts out her patients with beans three times a day, for major spring cleaning, then as their systems start to regulate, they can level off. For more information you can check out nutritionist Karen Hurd's website here: http://bit.ly/1h2x8zW.

I can't say I eat beans three times a day, but it's pretty good motivation to increase our consumption of them overall.

The Arguments Against Beans
(and Katie's Tips to Maximize Nutrition)

Although legumes have a fairly good reputation, there are always naysayers with warnings about a given food. Here are the most common reasons you'll hear people warn *against* eating beans and my thoughts on them:

1. *The iron in legumes isn't absorbed well by the human body.*
   Consuming legumes along with Vitamin C gives you a better chance of absorbing the iron, and even if the system isn't perfect for this one nutrient, I haven't heard that it hurts to have unabsorbed iron passing through. Many legume recipes already include tomatoes and colored peppers, which are high in Vitamin C, and including an orange or a side of broccoli with your dinner is another easy way to achieve this balance.

2. *Fiber isn't good for you.*
   Or is it? Some sources disdain fiber as a naughty nutrient. There's always an alternative opinion backed by research if you don't like what you read. However, if you're not a fan of fiber, sprouting your legumes can reduce the problems there.

3. *Beans aren't a complete protein.*
   There's another option to be easier on the budget and obtain adequate protein intake. Include some meat in lesser amounts instead of making a completely meatless meal. A meal with as little as 2% meat paired with beans allows the body to assimilate the vegetable protein completely. Bone broth will also extend the value of the animal protein you include in your menu, so a soup with a bit of meat and some beans is an excellent option. (http://www.kitchenstewardship.com/BoneBroth)

4. *Beans can be hard on digestion because of the phytic acid.*
   The overnight soaking process and the long cooking for legumes should sufficiently reduce the phytic acid for most people (see page 14 for instructions). If you have terrible mineral absorption issues or serious cavities, you may want to see if things get better without legumes, but for most of us, we're not going to avoid 100% of phytic acid anyway.

5. *Legumes have lots of carbs and will make you gain weight.*
   First, the carbohydrates in legumes are complex and paired with protein, so they're quite effective for losing weight overall. The friend I mentioned above lost ten pounds in a month by cutting grains and sugar and including legumes three times a day. Second, you can also reduce the overall carb load considerably by sprouting your beans.

6. *There are dangers to home-cooked kidney beans because of a toxic protein called phytohemagglutinin.*
   Yes, kidney beans can have a dangerous lectin that causes extreme intestinal distress if even a few beans are eaten raw, but soaking and boiling for just 10 minutes completely deactivates the toxin. I can't imagine that 4+ hours on your stove wouldn't be enough. It is sometimes recommended that one avoid the slow cooker method for kidney beans, if you'd like to play it safe. Just don't eat crunchy or sprouted, raw kidney or cannellini beans. [source: http://1.usa.gov/1peMRzM]

Canned vs. Dry Beans

Whether you choose canned beans, dry beans, or a blend of both depending on your time, energy and preparation foresight, beans are a frugal and nourishing choice.

	Pros	**Cons**
Dry Beans	Less money	More work (slightly)
	In control of ALL ingredients	Must pre-plan
	Long soak unlocks all the nutrients/health benefits	
	Less packaging waste	
	Avoid BPA in cans	
	Option to “toss in a bit more” in many recipes	
Canned Beans	Quick and easy!	Higher cost
	Most sources, other than the traditional foods paradigm, say canned beans are just fine nutritionally (unlike most canned foods, like vegetables)	Conservative sources say manufacturers' method of cooking makes them less nutritious, both in proteins and nutrients
		Might have added preservatives/salt
		More waste (cans)
		Exposure to BPA in cans

I default to dry beans almost 100% of the time these days. Using them can be simple, especially if you cook large batches and freeze the extras for those days that you haven't pre-planned a meal.

To price compare dry beans to canned, assume that you'll get about 5-7 cups of cooked beans from one pound of dry. A can is about 1 ½-2 cups of beans. That means a one pound bag will equal about 3-4 cans. I recommend checking value grocery stores like Aldi or Save-a-Lot for the best prices on both dry and canned beans, but be sure to also watch the sales at your regular grocery store.

What About Organic? Sometimes I buy organic dry legumes. I find them more likely to be higher quality, fresher, and have fewer questionable looking beans than the very inexpensive store brands. However, in general legumes aren't in the category of highest importance for purchasing organics. Grown inside a pod, the beans themselves aren't going to be exposed to sprays quite as often.

That said, sometimes organic is worth the price comparison. Because you might be able to find larger bulk sizes from health food stores or co-ops, it can be the case that organic legumes are equal to or only a slightly higher cost than their conventionally grown counterparts. If your budget is very tight, I wouldn't feel at all guilty about buying store brand beans, preferably on sale.

How to Use Canned Beans

Canned beans are already cooked, so you'll simply need to open the can, dump the contents into a strainer/colander, rinse gunk off thoroughly, and use in a recipe or cold. Most recipes you'll find will remind you to "drain and rinse" the beans, although the occasional recipe does include the liquid in the can (not in this book).

How to Cook Dry Beans

1. Measure and Rinse Dry Legumes

Decide the quantity of dry beans you need to cook. The recipes in this book all include the exact amount of dry beans for that recipe, so you can measure them dry. However, I highly recommend cooking in bulk, one to two pounds at a time, and simply using what you need for a recipe and freezing the remainder. Most recipes you find call for either a can (about 1 ¾ cups cooked beans) or give the *cooked* measurements.

Rinse the dry beans in a colander thoroughly under cool water while sorting through them for any stones or other debris. I've actually found a pebble and clumps of dirt before, so don't skip this step any more than you would eat lettuce from your garden without washing it. I also toss out any strange-looking or overly wrinkly beans. I don't trust them.

If you're using lentils, mung beans, or split peas, it's possible skip the soaking and cook them dry. However, if you want to really maximize your nutrition, include the next step anyway: soaking.

> **An important tip**: Choose a large pot. Dry beans expand quite a bit when soaked, which is why you need to really drown them in at least twice as much water, if not four times as much. The last thing you want to be cleaning up at breakfast is black bean liquid all over your stove top or counter because your pot overflowed! In other words, never fill your pot more than 1/3 of the way with dry beans.

2. Soak Dry Beans and Legumes

All dry beans and legumes, even though those mentioned above that *can* be cooked without a soak, *should* be soaked before cooking (see the section on "Why Soak Legumes" for details). Soaking shortens the cooking time and makes the beans more digestible.

To soak, cover the washed beans with four times their volume of water. The optimal soaking temperature is 140F, but I usually just use my hottest tap water. (*Note: I don't usually use hot tap water for cooking because of possible leaching in the pipes or hot water heater. However, this is the one place I'm often lazy. You might simply heat water in a teapot shy of boiling. Blend with cold water if you get it too hot.)*

Choose one of these soaking techniques:

1. *Nourishing soak*: Soak for 12-24 hours. The long soak is the healthier method and makes the beans more digestible. I write in my calendar to "soak beans" in the morning, then the following morning "cook beans" for dinner that night.
2. *Normal soak*: Leave the beans to soak for 4-8 hours or overnight.
3. *Quick soak*: (Less healthy, but works in a pinch) Bring the beans to a boil for one minute, cover, and let sit for one hour.

Note: Unlike soaking grains, you do not need any salt, vinegar, or lactic acid medium added to the soaking water. In fact, those may hinder the bean's softness.

I always soak right in the pot I'll use to cook the beans, which is often the pot I'll use for the final bean recipe. Why wash more dishes than necessary? You'll want to cover the pot while they soak if there's a chance of bugs or debris falling in, but in the winter I often leave the lid off out of laziness with no repercussions.

An option to reduce flatulence: It is said that if you pour off the water mid-soak and replace with fresh water, you can cut down on the flatulence sometimes blamed on beans and legumes. The traditional Mexican herb epazote may also help.

3. Cook Dry Beans and Legumes

Nourishing Cook (with soaking technique 1): Drain, rinse, and return the beans to the pot. Add water to cover beans twice as deep. Bring to a gentle boil and skim off any foam that appears. Reduce heat and simmer, covered, for 4-8 hours until soft. (It is said that simmering for the first hour or so *un*covered may reduce "wind.") *This is the method I use regularly.*

It is very important to note that a simmer for dry beans is a different beast than the "low heat" you want for something like rice. I cook beans somewhere between level 2 and 4 on my gas range's normal burner or about 2 on my larger "power" burner (5 is dead center). You don't need to see a rolling boil the whole time, but if steam is rising, that's a good sign that the water is hot enough. I put the lid on after the first hour or so (or the whole time if I'm not going to be around), and that really changes things. You might only want level 1-2 on your burner so that your water isn't bubbling away too furiously.

I always plan to start cooking the beans in the morning after breakfast, because it's okay if they're finished a little early. They'll wait for dinnertime just fine with the heat off, drained or undrained. If I don't have time in the morning or forget, I always figure the last possible chance is by the end of lunch or about 1:00. That way I know they'll be ready by dinner prep time. I do leave beans cooking on the stove when I'm out of the house, but that's certainly a choice to make at your own discretion.

Normal Cook (with soaking techniques 2 and 3): You have the choice of cooking in the soak water (more nutrients) or draining, rinsing and adding new water (less flatulence). Whether reusing soaking water or adding fresh, there should be twice as much water as beans. Boil furiously, uncovered, for ten minutes. Cover, lower heat, and simmer for 1-2 hours, until tender. *Note: this is the conventional way to cook beans often found on a bag of dry beans. It is NOT the method I use or recommend.*

Troubleshooting:

Unbelievably, some beans can cook for 8 hours and *still* be crunchy, which is very frustrating. Sometimes I throw up my hands, not wishing to risk failure, and just boil furiously for 10 minutes at the beginning of the cooking. If I'm patient enough, I remember to simply keep the temp at medium-low or so and check in before it's dinnertime and too late for a high boil intervention, only if necessary.

If your beans are crunchy after 6-8 hours, add a *pinch of baking soda* to the water and crank the heat up a bit. The one comfort in this process is that you can't burn them or irreparably mess them up! (Note: Beans that struggle to cook may split and look less than desirable for cold bean salads, but you can always use them in soups.)

The bonus element of cooking with dry beans is that although you have to address them the night before and during the day, when you're actually ready to cook and feeling the dinner hour rush, the dry beans are cooked and ready to go and you don't have to do anything to them.

Additional Tips:

- 1 cup dry beans yields 2-2½ cups cooked. Unless otherwise stated, the amounts in each recipe's ingredients list refer to the cooked volume (although I do provide dry bean measurements if you're not soaking and cooking in bulk).
- Both salt and acids (vinegar, lemon juice, tomatoes) can disrupt the cooking and result in crunchy beans, so do not add either one while soaking or during the first hour of cooking.
- Optional: When beans are softened, add 1 tsp. salt per cup of dry beans to the liquid and simmer until fully dissolved, or longer. This may "soften the carbs," according to cookbook author Rebecca Wood (http://bit.ly/LUtahp).
- When you drain the beans, get in the habit of putting something under the colander to reserve the cooking liquid. I use my 4-cup glass measuring cup. This way you're ready to use the nutrient-filled liquid in your recipe in place of any water called for and are prepared for those recipes that actually require the bean cooking liquid. (Note: If you're very wary of flatulence, you may want to simply use water instead of bean cooking liquid, which could possibly retain some of the gas-promoting qualities.)
- I like using a measuring cup to put beans back into my recipe right from the colander, usually estimating about two cups per can of beans required (the *precise* amount is really more like 1 ¾ cup, which is rarely important in soups, stews, casseroles, Mexican dishes, etc.). I use heaping cupfuls to boost the nutrition and stretch any recipe.
- I can use that same cup to measure out my extra beans for frozen storage.
- Links to slow cooker methods for beans:
  - A Year of Slow Cooking (http://bit.ly/1aA4FRC) (although she says to soak in the fridge if your climate is warm, which really isn't necessary)
  - GNOWFGLINS (http://bit.ly/LUts7X) (but skip the "add an acid" step)
  - I wouldn't recommend cooking kidney beans this way - although they're probably fine, there's some risk of them not getting hot enough to neutralize the toxin that's mainly only found in kidney beans. More info on p. 12, number six under "Arguments Against Beans."

Storing Cooked Beans

I cook at least a whole pound of dry beans and then freeze the leftovers in 1 1/2-2 cup servings for future recipes. My favorite containers are either glass pint jars, glass peanut butter jars, or plastic tubs from 16 oz. cottage cheese or sour cream. This is the perfect size for "one can" of beans. Of course, cool before putting into plastic containers, if using. Leave a little headroom before freezing, but it's not of utmost importance since there isn't liquid to expand.

Cooked beans can also survive in the fridge for about one week awaiting another recipe or for use in cold salads. If you leave them too long, believe me, you'll KNOW when they get bad!

Making Vegetable Broth

Cooking dry beans is a great opportunity to make a homemade, healthy vegetable broth if you need it for a recipe (or might within the next 6 months). It's so simple. While the beans cook, just add to the pot:

- 2-4 cloves unpeeled garlic
- 2 bay leaves
- 1-2 carrots, halved
- 1-2 celery ribs, halved
- a few leek greens (optional) or onions, in chunks

Season to taste with salt and pepper during the last 10-30 minutes of cooking time. You can also add epazote for flatulence or other herbs of your choice for flavor. When you drain the beans, remember to capture all the liquid in a large glass bowl. You can use it as a vegetable broth immediately or store in the freezer just like you would any liquid. Take care to leave at least an inch of headroom for expansion.

I like to freeze broth in 2- or 4-cup portions, labeled, so I don't have to play any guessing games or measure anything when I'm ready to use it. Glass quart jars or 16 oz. plastic tubs are ideal.

Pick the vegetables out of the beans and compost or throw them away; they've served their purpose and don't really have any nutritional value remaining. If it pains you to throw away food, think of them as empty vessels, more like packaging than real food any longer.

Keep in mind that the broth will take on the color of the beans, so if you want it for a light-colored soup like Tuscan Bean Soup (p. 53), don't use broth from black beans. Black bean broth melds seamlessly into meat-and-tomato-based chili and can also be used in place of water for the Veggie Bean Burritos on page 25.

Pressure Cooker Method

I hesitate to include this method, because some conservative sources claim that pressure-cooking beans reduces their nourishment, and in that case you might as well use cans. However, even pressure-cooked beans are still more frugal than cans, and in our household the option to use the pressure cooker was an important step in my transition to both using more beans and learning to manage bags of dry beans. Therefore, to use at your discretion, here are the basic steps (from the book *Pressure Perfect*):

- 1 lb. (about 2 ½ cups) dried beans, picked over and rinsed
- 9 c. water
- ¾ tsp. salt (add right at the start – enhances flavor and helps beans hold on to delicate skins and keep their shape)
- 1 Tbs. oil (needed to control foaming)

In a 6-qt or larger cooker, combine the beans, water, salt, and oil. I usually just use extra virgin olive oil because it's easy to pour.

Lock lid in place. Bring to high pressure by cooking over high heat. Reduce heat just enough to maintain high pressure and cook for the length of time indicated on Bean Timing Chart (next page). Turn off the heat and allow pressure to come down naturally, which will take 15 to 20 minutes. Remove the lid, tilting it away from you to allow steam to escape.

Test the beans for softness. If they are still a bit firm, replace (but do not lock) the lid and simply simmer until done. If they are really quite hard, lock the lid and return to high pressure for another minute to 5 minutes and again allow the pressure to come down naturally (i.e., do not run the pot under cold water to release the lid).

If time permits, allow the beans to cool in the cooking liquid, uncovered. (During this time, beans will firm up and any slightly underdone beans will complete cooking.) Drain in batches in a large colander. Avoid crushing the beans by piling them in a big heap.

Note: If using a 4-qt cooker, divide recipe in half but still use a full tablespoon of oil.

Bean Timing Chart for Pressure Cooking

For firm beans, to be served on their own or in salads, cook for the minimum suggested time. Allow 15-20 minutes for the natural pressure release, which is essential to completing the job properly. Also allow extra time for any additional cooking that may be needed. Always add 1 tablespoon of oil to control foaming; 2 tablespoons for limas. Do not fill the cooker more than halfway when cooking beans.

1 cup dried beans	**Minutes High Pressure w/ natural release**	**Yield in Cups**
Adzuki (Azuki)	16-21	2
Black (Turtle)	22-25	2
Black-Eyed Peas	6-8	2 ¼
Cannellini	28-32	2
Chickpeas (Garbanzos)	32-35	2 ½
Cranberry (Borlotti)	28-34	2 ¼
Flageolet	28-34	2
Great Northern	25-30	2 ¼
Lentils (brown or French green)	1 to 5 (after 1 minute high pressure, allow pressure to release naturally for 8 mins, then quick release any remaining.)	2
Lentils (red)	5 (red lentils do not hold their shape, so you can use quick-release method)	2
Lima (large)**Use 2 Tbs oil per 1 cup beans to control foaming.*	9-10	2 ½
Lima (baby)	13-15	2 ½
Navy (pea)	22-25	2
Peas (split, green or yellow)	10-12	2
Pinto	19-22	2 ¼
Red Kidney	25-30	2
Romano (Roman)	25-30	2
Small Red Beans	26-30	2

Why Soak Legumes?

Legumes are seeds, which means they are not designed to be digested but to be propagated. In the seed's great plan, they would rather pass through your system and get into the earth to sprout and grow a new plant. (Oh, my third graders used to love talking about this concept with great amounts of squirming!)

If we want to obtain all the awesome health benefits of beans, we need to battle their propensity for reproduction. Legumes contain anti-nutrients that make them difficult to digest and enzyme inhibitors that keep them from sprouting until the time is right.

The primary anti-nutrient, called phytic acid, is bound to many of the minerals in the legume, like calcium, iron, phosphorus and magnesium. The bean holds onto all that goodness and won't release it for your body unless you break down the phytate bond between the phytic acid and the minerals. The enzyme inhibitors that prevent the seed from sprouting can also hinder enzymatic activity in your digestive system, which happens to be run by enzymes. This is not a good thing.

Soaking beans overnight in hot water (about 140F is optimal) serves to reduce the anti-nutrients sufficiently for most people to enjoy the health benefits of beans without risking poor mineral absorption.

The other option is sprouting the beans, actually beginning the process of germination so that the beans no longer have a need for enzyme inhibitors and anti-nutrients.

How to Sprout Beans

Sprouting beans or legumes is actually quite simple and takes just a minute or two a day. The hardest part is planning ahead, because sprouting fully take 2-5 days, depending on the bean. You'll want to make a note in your calendar considerably before the night you want to cook with beans.

The basic process:

1. Rinse and soak legumes in a bowl of water for at least 12 hours. This water does not need to be hot like a normal soak. Be sure to cover the legumes with twice the amount of water as they will expand.

2. Drain into a colander.

3. Place a plate or small bowl under the colander to catch any water drips, and simply leave the legumes in the colander to sprout. Beware of trying to sprout more than a pound at a time as the beans can suffer from lack of air circulation and have mold problems.

4. Approximately every 12 hours (breakfast and dinner works great), rinse with clear water and set out again to keep sprouting.

5. In 24-72 hours, you should see sprouts! You can choose to cook them as soon as they sprout or when the sprout is 1/4" long or so. I've never sprouted longer than that, but it's certainly possible. The taste would likely increase in sweetness a bit.

6. More detailed directions and photographs can be found here: http://www.kitchenstewardship.com/MMSprout

Sprouted legumes can be cooked following normal cooking directions as if they had simply been soaked. They often take less time to cook. The taste is sometimes slightly different, usually a little sweeter, but in a sweet lettuce or carrot sort of way rather than sugary.

Sprouted legumes have lots of additional health benefits:

- Lower carbohydrates and fewer calories (because the seed has started consuming some of its own starchy "food" in the cotyledon and is becoming a small plant)
- Increased Vitamins A and C
- Reduced anti-nutrients for better mineral absorption
- Less fiber
- Lower glycemic load
- more: http://www.kitchenstewardship.com/WhySprout

Even though sprouting legumes takes very little time, it still commandeers a space in your kitchen and dirties a dish. As with most processes, I recommend sprouting as much as your colander can handle and freezing the extras. Particularly in the case of lentils, which are very easy to sprout and cook, there are many uses for leftovers!

Menu Planning for Beans

I highly recommend including beans and legumes in your weekly menu plan regularly. This doesn't necessarily mean you need a bean-based main dish once a week, although that's not a bad idea for your waist or budget. You can incorporate more beans into your diet by adding them in such dishes as:

- ✓ Salsa
- ✓ Salads
- ✓ Eggs
- ✓ Egg salad (mashed white beans, a small amount)
- ✓ Any Mexican dish
- ✓ Meat-based wraps for extra flavor/filler
- ✓ Refried beans on a grilled cheese sandwich

For babies and toddlers, cooked beans make surprisingly simple finger foods. I loved being able to scatter a few beans on the high chair tray while I prepared the rest of the meal, and I even recall having a bowl of black beans at church once or twice! Just smash them flat if you're really concerned about them sliding down your child's throat.

And if you really don't like beans (or have a family member in that category)? Some hidden bean tricks:

- ✓ Pureed white beans in mashed potatoes
- ✓ Sometimes mashed bean dips like hummus can get people past the texture of whole, cooked beans. It's worth experimenting and using lots of flavor!
- ✓ Blending beans up (white is usually best) to thicken a creamy soup or even a hearty chicken noodle
- ✓ Mashed beans in spaghetti sauce (kidney would hide best; start with a half can or less, about ½ cup)
- ✓ Recipes in this book that don't taste like beans: Dosas (p. 35), Mexican Black Bean Burgers (p. 30), Chickpea Wraps (p. 27) - fry them thin and crispy! and both pasta recipes with blended white beans as a sauce (p. 69 and 71).
- ✓ Hidden lentils (see below)
- ✓ You can also try pureeing the beans in any recipe and see what happens, if the texture of beans is your hang up.

Many of the recipes in this book include suggestions for other recipes to use in the same week, both to serve alongside the meal and to help use up extra beans, spinach, or other perishables that a given recipe may require. I love connecting my meal planning together so that I can do some work on one day and reap the benefits another day.

Cooking with Lentils (and Hiding Them)

A lot of people who have never tried green lentils ask me what they taste like. Alone, they don't taste that great, actually. However, kind of like the soy products that claim to taste like meat and cheese and everything else, lentils are a fairly blank slate that can take on other flavors around them. They also mash really well and don't have a vibrant color. They're perfect for the unsuspecting bean hater.

Lentils are a great stretcher food, meaning that they can sneak into dishes with ground beef when you don't want to use as much meat simply because it's expensive. There's nothing unhealthy about good, grassfed red meat, but we need to balance our physical health with the health of our bank account.

Sneaky Food? I don't advocate being sneaky too often with food, because I do think it's important for kids (and adults) to appreciate their palates and understand what they're eating and why. However, if someone in your family hates beans like we hate liver, you can still help them benefit from beany nutrition. (I hide liver in lots of dishes, but I'll tell you it's there if you ask!)

Although the package directions will say otherwise, lentils should still be soaked overnight for digestibility, but they cook much quicker than most legumes (about 30 minutes). I freeze them in plastic bags in one-or-two-cup portions and can incorporate them into a meal even if I've forgotten to thaw them. Once cooked, try adding lentils to:

- ✓ Tacos: *Use a 1:1 ratio with meat, although you may want to start with less. Be sure to use the amount of taco seasoning you'd need for the total mass, not just the weight of the meat.*
- ✓ Sloppy Joes: *same instructions as above*
- ✓ Spaghetti with meat sauce
- ✓ Meatballs and Meatloaf: *Start out easy and work up to the point where you still can't taste them and the meatloaf doesn't lose its texture. Make sure you have enough seasonings/spices in your meat mix. (http://www.kitchenstewardship.com/Meatloaf)*
- ✓ Any ground-beef based casserole or Italian pasta bake
- ✓ Any Mexican meal with ground beef

Well-sprouted lentils are also a fun topping for cold salads and can actually be eaten raw. They make a pretty decent and unique salad by themselves, with a nice vinaigrette and some chopped vegetables.

Here are some other lentil recipes if you find yourself becoming a fan:

- ✓ Lentil Spaghetti (http://bit.ly/1aA6uxV)
- ✓ Sweet & Sour Lentils (http://bit.ly/1g7jvgt)
- ✓ French Lentil Salad (http://bit.ly/1l1ssek)
- ✓ Lentil Vegetable Pottage (a yummy, Candida-fighting soup) (http://bit.ly/1bzmM8A)
- ✓ 3 Dishes From Sprouted Lentils (http://bit.ly/MvBeFb)
- ✓ Ginger, Chicken, Rice & Lentil Stew (http://bit.ly/1eCitKR)
- ✓ Minty Beef & Lentil Stew (http://bit.ly/1lDMUWq)
- ✓ Sloppy Joes In A Bowl (http://bit.ly/1eYQdyp)
- ✓ Garden Lentil Patties (http://bit.ly/1eYQe5t)
- ✓ Mujadarah (Arabic Lentil & Brown Rice Stew) (http://bit.ly/1lDMY8F)

A Note About Soy

Soy is an extremely controversial food right now. You can find many sources that praise soybeans as the only legumes that are a complete protein. You can also find sources that say soy of any kind is simply unsafe to eat unless it is fermented. For me, I'm wary enough to simply stay away from soybeans.

The one bag of dry soybeans I bought when I read the "soy is healthy" information has been repurposed into learning activities for my kids. From what I understand, soybeans are tough to cook with and stink up the house, anyway!

Veggie Bean Burritos

Work Intensity Kid-Friendly Cost

This is really an any-time-of-year kind of recipe, from utilizing garden bounty in the summer to fitting perfectly with sales at the grocery store throughout the winter. Since you can swap veggies in and out, it's incredibly versatile and delicious every time.

Ingredients GF CF

If soaking dry beans, start with 2 cups before soaking.

For the sauce:

2-4 Tbs. water or olive oil
1 small onion, chopped
1 clove garlic, crushed
1 small can green chiles OR ~1/2-1 chopped jalapeno, seeded
½ T. chili powder
½ tsp. ground cumin
¼ tsp. ground coriander (optional, or use cilantro)
dash cayenne
8 oz. can tomato sauce (1 cup)
¼ c. tomato paste
1 c. water

For the filling:

2-4 Tbs. water or olive oil
1 small onion, chopped
2 ½ c. chopped veggies (green pepper, corn, zucchini, fresh mushrooms)
2 cans black beans, drained and rinsed, OR 3-4 c. cooked
½ c. water
1 tsp. chili powder
½ tsp. cumin

6-8 large tortillas
shredded cheese (optional)

Method

To make sauce: Use a small saucepan over medium heat. In water or olive oil, sauté onion and jalapeno (if using) for about 5 minutes, adding garlic at the last minute. Add canned chiles (if using) and spices, stir and sauté a few minutes. Add remaining sauce ingredients, mix well and simmer about 15 minutes.

To make filling: Over medium heat in a large pot, sauté onion, green pepper, and mushrooms in water or oil for about 5 minutes, until onions are translucent. Toss in everything else and cook 10 more minutes, stirring occasionally.

You can just fill the tortillas with the hot filling and eat smothered with sauce, or make baked burritos. Put a little sauce in the bottom of 9×13 pan, put the filling in tortillas, top with more sauce and cheese and bake 15-30 minutes at 350 degrees F.

Serves 4-6.

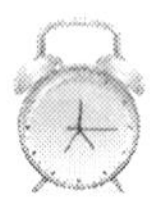

Timesaver: I almost always end up with twice as many vegetables as I need – it doesn't take much chopping to get 2 ½ cups! – so I double the filling recipe, and a single batch of sauce covers it all.

Added Bonus: You eat a lot of vegetables in what feels like a pretty traditional Mexican meal.

Substitutions and Frugal Tips

- ✓ Any vegetables you have on hand could be used in this recipe. I often skip the corn to decrease the carbs, and adding a few handfuls of spinach to the cooked vegetables goes nearly undetected.
- ✓ Make your own 100% whole wheat tortillas to increase nutrition and decrease cost. Here's my recipe: http://bit.ly/4cpJEr
- ✓ *Frugal tip:* Watch for organic mushrooms on sale – they're often priced the same as conventionally grown mushrooms. I make this dish when I can get the mushrooms, and I always have chopped zucchini and peppers (both spicy and sweet) in my freezer from the Farmer's Market. (How to freeze: http://www.kitchenstewardship.com/FreezerPrep) You can also watch reduced produce sections for both zucchini and peppers.
- ✓ *Easy gluten-free*: just use corn tortillas or dosas (p. 35), or serve over cooked brown rice as a "burrito bowl."
- ✓ This meal hardly needs a side dish, but Mexican Rice and Beans (p. 61) or Refried Beans (p. 57) with a salad complete it nicely for a crowd.

FAQs

- ✓ *What do I do with the rest of the can of tomato paste?* I recommend freezing the rest for the next batch, since ¼ cup is about half a 6 oz. can. You can freeze the paste in 1 Tbs. "plops" on a cookie sheet for those odd recipes that call for just a little bit of tomato paste, like some beef stews, Russian dressing, or Cuban Black Beans Over Rice (p. 67).
- ✓ *What if I don't have the right tomatoes?* You can sub 1 14-oz. can of diced tomatoes for both the tomato paste and sauce, although I prefer the original.
- ✓ *Does it freeze?* Yes! Both sauce and filling, separately, freeze excellently.
- ✓ *Is it spicy?* Not really. I highly recommend tasting both sauce and filling before serving, and don't be afraid to increase the spices. Then again, if you have a very "mild" family with young children, shoot low on the chili powder and go from there.

Chickpea Wraps

With a tangy dose of mustard and mayo or ranch dressing, the crunch of lettuce, some melted cheese, and perhaps some red onion for a truly delightful zip, you almost forget you're sacrificing meat when you eat these nourishing, frugal wraps.

Ingredients GF CF

If soaking dry beans, start with ¾ cups before soaking.

2 Tbs. olive oil
1½ c. onions, minced
3 cloves garlic, minced
1 tsp. ground cumin
1 c. carrot, finely chopped or shredded
1¾ c. cooked and drained chickpeas (about 1 can)
1½ Tbs. tahini or peanut butter
¼ c. fresh parsley, minced, or 1 Tbs. dried
1/3 c. white or whole wheat flour or chickpea flour
½ tsp. baking soda
1 tsp. salt

Method

If you have a food processor, make it work for you. Process the onions just enough to get them chopped, then sauté them in oil for about five minutes. (I tend to use the pan I know I'll want for frying the patties, which is my cast iron. Saves a dish!) Meanwhile, shred carrots in your food processor to fill one cup and toss in the garlic to mince it, too. (You can use the regular blade to chop/shred the carrots.) Garlic's health benefits are best five minutes after mincing, so try chopping the cloves first, remove the minced garlic, then process the carrots. Add the carrots and cumin to the onions for a minute, then the garlic for one last minute, stirring frequently.

If using fresh parsley, process it before the chickpeas to get it evenly chopped. Process the cooked chickpeas (garbanzo beans) into a paste, then add the sauteed vegetables and process until fully incorporated. Don't be alarmed if the chickpeas look dry by themselves; the sauteed veggies add enough moisture for a real "paste." Stir or process in peanut butter/tahini and parsley.

Combine the flour, baking soda, and salt in a small bowl, then stir into the mixture in the food processor.

Preheat a skillet and add some healthy oil like coconut oil or tallow to fry the patties. Form the paste into patties either using a spatula against the side of your bowl or simply by dropping heaping tablespoonfuls into the hot oil, then pressing them down a bit to flatten. If you only have extra virgin olive oil on hand, keep the temperature on low to medium low and adjust the time accordingly.

Fry small, thin patties in the hot oil over medium-high heat for 4-5 minutes, until just beginning to brown (check them after 2 minutes to see how the progress is going). Turn over and fry the other side until browned; crispy is optimal. Sometimes I decide to flip them a couple of times to get a nice brown crunch. The whole process takes about 10 minutes per batch. You'll likely need to add additional oil between batches, especially if you're using a cast iron skillet.

Serve warm in tortillas. We enjoy shredded cheese, mustard and mayo (http://www.kitchenstewardship.com/MayoVlog), ranch dressing (http://www.kitchenstewardship.com/RanchDressing), and lots of lettuce on top. Red onion is also delightful.

Serves 4-6 adults, depending on your side dish options. Makes about twenty 3" patties.

Timesaver: Shred cheese for your freezer before making this recipe, then you won't have to wash the food processor twice.

Added Bonus: The recipe makes a lot more than you'd expect for one little can of beans, and it actually freezes great! Freeze some of the uncooked filling along with extra tortillas, then thaw the filling and fry up for a super simple meal later (I recommend a double batch).

Substitutions and Frugal Tips

- ✓ *Substitution ideas*: You could easily sneak a few more veggies in, like gently steamed spinach or fresh red peppers. Once you're putting dinner into a food processor anyway, it's a great time to hide some nutrient-packed extras!
- ✓ Try homemade whole wheat tortillas to keep the nutrition up and the cost down. (http://www.kitchenstewardship.com/WWTortilla)

- ✓ We like to serve with homemade chicken rice-a-roni (p. 64) or cheesy rice and tomatoes (http://www.kitchenstewardship.com/CheesyRice), steamed vegetables and a salad. To complete the Mediterranean undertones in the meal, try homemade Greek dressing. (http://www.kitchenstewardship.com/GreekDressing)

FAQs

- ✓ *What if I don't have a food processor?* You can use a hand blender or even a potato masher to smash the chickpeas and simply stir in the remaining ingredients. Be sure to finely chop the onions and shred or very finely chop the carrots if you don't have a tool to blend them into the mixture.

- ✓ *What's the gluten-free alternative?* Try a GF flour in the patties or chickpea flour. I have tried arrowroot starch, but it just didn't *thicken* and turned into a gloppy mess in the pan.

- ✓ *No peanut butter?* For those with nut allergies or babies not yet introduced to peanut butter, simply skip that ingredient. The meal is still great without it!

Recipe adapted from The Veggie Table (http://bit.ly/1ofFrM6).

Mexican Black Bean Burgers

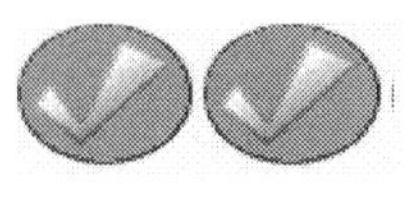

Work Intensity Kid-Friendly Cost

A little Mexican flair and some fun toppings take veggie burgers from "boring" to "wow!" Make them without the spicy parts and use traditional burger toppings for a great fake-out grilled burger.

Ingredients

CF If soaking dry beans, start with 1 cup before soaking.

1 small onion, quartered
1/2 red pepper, cut into a few pieces
3 garlic cloves, peeled
2 jalapenos, seeds removed or ½-2 tsp. cayenne pepper *(to taste! Cut way down if serving kids…)*
2 c. cooked black beans (or one can, drained and rinsed)
1 1/2 c. cooked green lentils
1/4 c. fresh cilantro (or 2 tsp. dry) (optional)
1 1/2 tsp. salt
1/2 tsp. pepper
2 eggs
1 ½ c. bread crumbs (plus more if needed)

Method

Allow legumes to cool if you just cooked them. Pulse the onion, pepper(s), optional fresh cilantro and garlic in a food processor until chopped. Add all the beans and lentils and process until pasty. If your food processor is a bit weak, you may want to tackle this in two batches.

When mostly smooth, add salt and pepper, dry cilantro and cayenne (if using), and the eggs. Process until combined and then add a cup of bread crumbs and process briefly until incorporated. Give a little stir around the very center for anything your blade may have missed. If your food processor is on the small side, you may wish to remove the legume/vegetable mixture to a bowl and simply stir in the rest of the ingredients.

Add more bread crumbs bit by bit until the mixture starts sticking together and pulls away from the center blade. It will be slightly stickier than you expect, but if you can spoon it without drips, you're on the right track.

Put some flour in a salad bowl to use in flouring your hands and the outside of the patties. Form 1/2- to 3/4-inch thick patties. The patties might seem a little fragile, but you don't want them too stiff or they might dry out and get crumbly once cooked.

Cook in a well-greased skillet over medium to medium-high heat, about 5-8 minutes on each side, turning at least once for even doneness. You can add oil in between sides, especially if you want a nice even browning look, or if you're using a cast iron skillet.

Serve as you would hamburgers. We like pretty standard toppings like mustard, ketchup, red onion, lettuce and pickles. Keep with the Mexican theme and offer fresh peppers, pickled jalapenos, avocado slices and salsa. If you skip the spices, these aren't fabulous to eat plain, but dressed up, they're ready for a party!

Makes 6-8 patties, 3-4" wide.

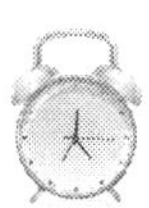

Timesaver: Make a large batch of lentils and freeze the extras to add to many dishes (see p. 23). I recommend trying to have either the beans or lentils (or both) prepared before the day you want to make the burgers.

Substitutions and Frugal Tips

- ✓ *Substitution ideas*: If you don't have lentils or are a "canned bean" person, you can use pintos in a pinch, but they definitely taste more "beany." The lentils are a better blank palette for the other flavors.

- ✓ How to make your own bread crumbs: http://www.kitchenstewardship.com/BreadCrumbs

- ✓ If you make your own bread crumbs, dry out the bread and process into crumbs just before beginning this recipe. You can also process the vegetables you might need for other side dishes, like the Chicken rice-a-roni imposter on page 64, further saving dishes and time.

FAQs

- ✓ *Extra beans?* Don't shoot high on the beans on this recipe! Unlike soups and burritos, use a scant measure if anything for something like this.
- ✓ Someday I'll try cooking these in a George Foreman. I think it would work well if the weight wasn't too much for the patties to bear.
- ✓ *What if I don't have a food processor?* A mini chopper makes this recipe tedious, but possible. A blender would have potential, if you just used it to puree the beans in small batches, perhaps with the egg, and then mixed everything in a large bowl.
- ✓ *I don't like the sharp flavor of the raw onions in the patties.* Just saute the onions (and peppers) before adding them to the processed mixture.
- ✓ *Can I freeze?* Yes! Freeze patties before frying.

Adapted from True Adventures in Money Hacking (http://bit.ly/1fdkUAi).

Spicy Turkey Chili Burgers

Work Intensity Kid-Friendly Cost

These gooey, cheesy burgers have always received rave reviews, especially from the men - is there some innate sense of satisfaction from biting into a thick, spicy piece of meat built into their genes?

Ingredients GF

If soaking dry beans, start with 1 cup before soaking.

¼ c. chili powder
2 Tbs. ground cumin
2 Tbs. grill seasoning, such as McCormick's Montreal Steak Seasoning
20 oz. package ground turkey breast
1 medium onion, finely chopped
2 Tbs. Worcestershire sauce
1 8-oz. can tomato sauce
1 can black or kidney beans, drained and rinsed, or 2 c. cooked beans
¼-½ of 1 red pepper, finely chopped
2 garlic cloves, minced
6 oz. cheddar (I prefer sharp), cut into ¼-in. dice
¼ c. refined coconut oil (or other heat stable fat)

Method

Combine the chili powder, cumin, and grill seasoning in a small bowl. Brown 1/4-1/5 of the turkey in a smallish pot over medium heat. When nearly finished, season with half of the spice mixture, then add half of the chopped onions and cook for another couple of minutes. When the onions are translucent, add the Worcestershire Sauce, tomato sauce and beans; bring up to a near-boil and then simmer the chili sauce over low heat until ready to serve.

Meanwhile, make the burgers. Place the remaining turkey in a bowl and add the remaining spice mixture, the remaining chopped onions, the red pepper, and garlic. Prep the cheese and a plate for the burger patties and/or the pan so you only have to get messy once. Mix well with your hands, then incorporate the diced cheese. Form the mixture into 4-6 patties, each about one inch thick.

Heat a skillet over med-high heat. Add a tablespoon of oil, more if using cast iron, and when hot, add the burgers. Cook the burgers for 6-12 minutes on each side or until no pink is left in the center. Serve on buns topped with the chili sauce.

Makes 4-6 patties.

Added Bonus: Since you'll only need about half or less of the chili sauce to top the burgers, a side dish is brain-dead easy. Just make a batch of brown rice and mix with the extra chili – instant beans and rice! Add a side veg and your meal is taken care of.

Timesaver: You can freeze cooked brown rice and quickly heat for a meal like this. I like to freeze convenient half-cup portions which are about one serving with stir fry or rice and beans.

Substitutions and Frugal Tips

- ✓ *Substitution ideas:* No reason you can't use beef here.
- ✓ *Frugal tip:* Watch for sales on ground turkey and freeze just for this recipe. It's worth it!
- ✓ You can make the chili in advance and simmer it on low all afternoon and keep the burger patties in the fridge if your mealtimes are hectic.
- ✓ Extra chili and no rice? Extra burger buns? Try "sloppy joes" with the chili sauce for another night in your week.

FAQs

- ✓ *Is there MSG in steak seasoning?* Possibly. If you're worried about it, you could just add a heaping teaspoon of coarsely ground sea salt, 1/2-1 tsp. black pepper, a pinch-1/4 tsp. red pepper, 1/2 tsp. of paprika and some extra garlic, or try skipping it altogether.
- ✓ *Are the burgers spicy?* Quite. Go easy on the spices if you're a "mild" family.

Recipe adapted from Rachael Ray 365: No Repeats – a Year of Deliciously Different Dinners.

Dosas

Dosas are a traditional Indian pancake-style wrap used more like a pita or tortilla. Soaked, ground, and fermented, the nutrition of the simple rice & lentils can't be beat.

Ingredients GF

2 c. brown rice
1 c. dry green lentils
3 c. water
3 Tbs. whey or yogurt
1 c. plain yogurt
1 c. water
1 tsp. sea salt
chopped fresh parsley (optional)
1 inch gingerroot, shredded (optional)
olive oil, coconut oil, or fat of choice for frying

Method

Soak rice and lentils in 3 cups water and whey or yogurt overnight (or at least 7 hours) at room temperature. I soak right in the blender to save dishes, but if you're worried about your metal blender blade reacting, you can use a covered bowl.

Strain water off. Add 1 cup yogurt and grind into a batter. Unless you have a high-powered blender, I recommend the following tips:

- Do half a batch at a time.
- Use a very low speed.
- Push the mixture down and around the blades, multiple times, with a spoon or spatula.
- Resist the urge to add more liquid until you've given it a minute or two and 4-5 manual stirs. You may think it will never work, and suddenly it will.

After everything is finally incorporated, mix on a medium-low speed for a minute or two to make sure you don't end up with hard little chunks. Put the batter in a large bowl or leave in the blender, and allow to ferment on the counter 24-48 hours, covered. The batter should be just barely pourable.

When ready to cook, add 1 cup lukewarm water to thin the batter. Add salt, chopped parsley and grated ginger to the batter. Stir well or blend for a minute.

Use a griddle heated to 350F or a skillet on medium-high to high, and ladle about ¼+ cup at a time to fry in oil like a pancake. Use the ladle to spread the batter out wide and thin. Flip when bubbles appear on the surface, very similar to a pancake. You'll also notice dry edges. If the batter is not thin enough, you can add a little water.

For a good substitute for a tortilla or pita, just leave out the ginger and parsley. There is a bit of a fermented taste, but once filled, you hardly notice.

Serve with a dip like hummus or a chutney (http://bit.ly/M8OVdp), or use like a tortilla to make any sort of wrap or taco meal. Once they're filled with ham, cheese and mustard, or chicken fajitas, the plain version blends right into the meal. What a way to hide the legumes!

Store leftovers in the refrigerator.

Makes about 10-14 6" rounds.

Added Bonus: Dosas are an easy gluten-free option for tortillas and pitas and can be stuffed with just about anything!

Substitutions and Frugal Tips

- ✓ *Substitution ideas:* I'm sure experimenting with various spices would open up a whole new world of seasoned wraps. I really prefer a plain version with the goal of dressing them up with various fillings.

FAQs

- ✓ *How do they reheat?* Dosas are definitely best fresh, but once stored, you can reheat them with a quick fry in a dry pan OR in a low-temp oven or toaster oven. They do crack and break if you try to wrap filling without heating them up.

This recipe is from Wild Fermentation *by Sandor Ellis Katz.*

Sausage, Bean and Greens Soup

This soup is fantastic in summer or winter and we make it often when spinach is abundantly on sale at the grocery. However, it's the dipping sandwiches that make the meal really special, so use summer tomatoes and local veggies for an A-1 rating!

Ingredients GF CF

If soaking dry beans, start with 1 ¾-2 cups before soaking.

1/2 or 1 lb. bulk Italian sweet or hot sausage
1 medium onion, chopped
2-3 carrots, chopped
1 large potato, cubed
2 cloves garlic, minced
1 bay leaf
2 cans white beans, drained and rinsed, or 4 c. cooked beans
1-2 tsp. salt (if using homemade broth)
1/4 tsp. pepper
4 c. fresh kale, spinach, or your favorite leafy green
2 quarts chicken broth or stock
Grated Parmigiano-Reggiano or Romano, to pass at table

Method

Heat a large soup pot and brown the sausage over medium heat. Add onion and saute a few minutes until softened. You can add some extra oil if the sausage didn't create enough grease. Add the rest of the veggies, bay leaf and beans. Season to taste with salt and pepper. Cook 5 minutes to soften veggies. Add greens and wilt with the cover on, 5 minutes or less. Pour in the stock and bring to a boil over high heat, covered. Reduce heat and simmer 15 minutes. Serve with grated Parmesan cheese.

Serves 6-8.

The amazing sandwich dipper: *Prepare to be amazed at how sophisticated grilled cheese gets when it grows up.* Use your favorite hearty bread with mozzarella, sliced tomatoes and fresh basil or pesto. Brush the outsides with olive oil. Grill as grilled cheese and serve hot. Thou must dip!

Substitutions and Frugal Tips

- ✓ Add even more flavor to the sandwiches with a quick dust of garlic powder on the outside after brushing with EVOO.
- ✓ We like to use our George Foreman to grill sandwiches with no flipping and no mess.
- ✓ *Frugal tips:* I usually use only half a pound of meat and find that the taste is quite sufficient. I save the other half, cooked, for a quick pasta or spaghetti sauce meal, for egg omelets, or for this Sausage Spinach Pasta Toss (http://www.kitchenstewardship.com/SausagePastaToss) or Sausage Zucchini Bake (http://www.kitchenstewardship.com/SausageZucchiniBake).

FAQs

- ✓ *Can I use roll sausage?* Sure! Just snip open the ends and squeeze the sausage out or slice and gently brown on both sides.
- ✓ *How can I make this a kosher meal?* Pork is certainly not necessary for a good sausage. You can make any ground meat into a tasty sausage substitute by following the directions here: http://www.kitchenstewardship.com/HomemadeSausage. Adjust spice to taste with cayenne.
- ✓ *Can I leave the skins on the potatoes?* I usually do for added iron, especially if organic.
- ✓ *What do I do with the rest of the bag of spinach?* You can lightly steam spinach and freeze it in ice cube trays for green smoothies (http://www.kitchenstewardship.com/GreenSmoothies), or plan another meal for the week to use up the bag. Some of our favorites include:
  *Tuscan Bean Soup (p. 53)
  *Beef and Bean Stew a la Tuscany (p. 75)
  *Sausage Spinach Pasta Toss
  http://www.kitchenstewardship.com/SausagePastaToss)
  *In scrambled eggs (http://www.kitchenstewardship.com/ScrambledEggs)
  *Sneak into many other soups, casseroles, or wraps
  *other places to stash spinach:
  http://www.kitchenstewardship.com/MMSpinach
- ✓ Super freezer friendly recipe!

Katie's Spicy Meat Chili

This is one of those recipes that is always slightly different. I've adapted it over and over through the years from a recipe that was delicious, but not exactly nutritious. I've gotten rid of all the processed canned ingredients in favor of whole foods, but it's still a very easy, inexpensive meal.

Ingredients GF CF

If soaking dry, start with ¾ c. kidneys and 1 ½ c. pintos.

1 lb. ground beef or venison or turkey
1 large onion, chopped
2 cloves garlic, minced OR 1/4 tsp. garlic powder
1 can kidney beans, drained and rinsed, or 2 c. cooked beans
2 cans pinto beans, drained and rinsed, or 4 c. cooked beans
1 6-oz. can tomato paste (optional)
15-oz. can diced tomatoes, undrained
8 oz. can tomato sauce
1 tsp. salt
1/4-1/2 tsp. pepper
1-3 Tbs. chili powder or a hot chili pepper or three, minced

Method

In a large pot, brown meat, onion and garlic. Cover with water, bring to a boil, and simmer, uncovered, for 20 minutes. (Covering with water literally just means to add water until the meat is all covered, less or more depending on how soupy you like your chili. If you love your measuring cups, 2-2 ½ cups should do it.) Add all the rest of the ingredients and bring to a boil again. Simmer for 30 minutes to let all the flavors blend.

Serves 6-8.

Substitutions and Frugal Tips

- ✓ *Substitution ideas:* Add a chopped green or red pepper or other healthy veggies as you wish. (Be aware that a green pepper really will change the flavor; I wrote a note to self on my recipe card not to use green again, for my personal tastes.) Pureed sweet potato or squash hides very well, and you can get inspiration from checking out the next recipe also.

- ✓ Easily get away with cutting the meat in half, or better yet, use a whole pound and then double everything else and freeze the leftovers.
- ✓ Don't have the right tomatoes? Stewed can go in place of diced, you can skip the paste completely, and you could add another pint of diced tomatoes in place of the tomato sauce if you're out.
- ✓ Try chicken stock or bean liquid in place of the water.
- ✓ It's a perfect recipe to add in some ground beef heart or liver if you're trying to eat more organ meats. See how: http://www.kitchenstewardship.com/Liver

FAQs

- ✓ *Where can I find canned tomatoes without BPA in the can linings?* A few companies offer tomato products in glass jars. I use Bionature, and Eden Foods is another option.
- ✓ *Isn't this a pretty spicy recipe?* Well, yes. You might want to start with even less chili powder than called for and taste as you go.
- ✓ *How do I use hot chili peppers in place of chili powder?* This was one of those real food revelations for me last summer at the Farmer's Market. Chili powder comes from...drum roll, please...dried chili peppers! When the farmer selling me a pint of chili peppers – the kind on the restaurant logo for Chili's – told me he used them to season chili and just skipped the powder, I was so surprised. I was just buying them because they were so darn cute!

  Now I have a little jar of chili peppers, all dried out, and I can roughly chop them/smash them and add to chili. Remember that the seeds are the hot part. I'd recommend starting with just one, seeded, to start. Let it cook 5-10 minutes before tasting to get the flavor and heat into the chili, and then adjust from there. The depth and richness of flavor is amazing, I'm telling you.
- ✓ *So...how do you dry out chili peppers?* I used my Excalibur dehydrator for just an hour or two, if I remember right, but you can even just hang them or lay them out to dry on the countertop. Keep them from getting wet and make sure they have air circulation, and wait 3-5 days until totally crispy.

Turkey Vegetable Chili

Work Intensity Kid-Friendly Cost

Unless people are really looking, they hardly notice how veggie-packed this massive, frugal pot of soup is. I feel great feeding it to my family to get winter veggies in them!

Ingredients

GF CF If soaking dry beans, start with ¾-1 cups *each* before soaking.

1 lb. ground turkey
2 Tbs olive oil
1 ½ c. minced onion
3 cloves minced garlic
1 ½ tsp. oregano
½ tsp. basil
2 Tbs. chili powder
½ tsp. cumin
¼ tsp. cayenne pepper
2 c. zucchini, washed, unpeeled, finely chopped
1 c. carrots, finely chopped
1 green pepper, chopped
1-2 red peppers, chopped
optional: spinach or other leafy green, washed and chopped
1 can (15 oz.) garbanzo beans, drained and rinsed, or 2 c. cooked
1 can (15 oz.) kidney beans, drained and rinsed, or 2 c. cooked
5 c. diced tomatoes with juice (~1 large & 1 small can, or 2 or 3 15-oz. cans)
3-4 c. water or broth (choose from chicken or turkey stock or the bean cooking water)

Method

In a large soup pot, brown ground meat over medium heat. Drain grease if necessary. Add oil and sauté onion until tender, adding fresh garlic just at the end. Season with spices, mix well. Add all vegetables and cook and stir a few minutes. Add beans, tomatoes and water or broth and stir. Bring to a boil. Reduce heat and simmer 45 minutes.

Serves 6.

Timesaver: You could certainly brown the meat and saute onion in the morning and crockpot this on low all day.

Added Bonus: This makes a whole bunch and is also very frugal. Great with homemade bread (http://www.kitchenstewardship.com/HomemadeBread), cornbread (http://www.kitchenstewardship.com/KSCornbread) or biscuits (http://www.kitchenstewardship.com/Biscuits). Also works with a grilled cheese sandwich for dipping.

Substitutions and Frugal Tips

- ✓ *Substitution ideas:* You can switch out almost any of the vegetables for something else, depending on what you have on hand.
- ✓ Add more beans! This is really quite a bean-light dish with only two cans. I highly recommend adding at least one more can of any sort of bean or just doubling what's called for. You won't regret it.
- ✓ A reviewer tried wrapping leftovers (after boiling down a bit) in tortillas with cheese. Yummy lunch!

FAQs

- ✓ *Is it spicy?* This is sort of a middle ground recipe. If you double the beans, it would likely end up on the mild end of the spectrum. Always taste the spices to see what you think, and don't be afraid to go shy on the heat or add more according to your family's tastes.
- ✓ *How much water? I like measuring cups!* As you add the water or broth, pay attention to how you like your chili. If you're looking for a deep, thick chili, stick with only two or three cups liquid. If you're okay with a spicy garden vegetable soup, go with all four cups.
- ✓ *Can I use other meats?* You could also use shredded chicken or leftover Thanksgiving turkey if you don't have access to ground turkey. The flavor is lighter than a traditional beef chili, so white meat is the perfect complement. Shoot for 2-3 cups of meat. Ground beef or venison would be great too.
- ✓ *Can I use less meat or go meatless?* I often make this recipe with half the ground meat called for, and I feel certain it would be lovely without the meat entirely.
- ✓ Freezes just great. Go for the double recipe!
  Recipe originally from a local heart health magazine.

White Chicken Chili with Lime

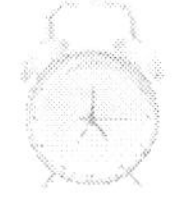
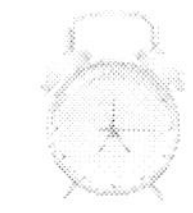
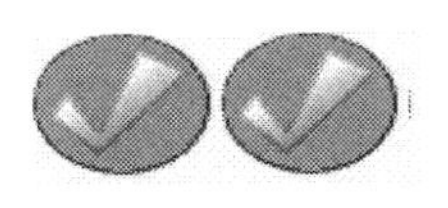

Work Intensity Kid-Friendly Cost

This is the recipe that introduced me to cumin and helped me fall in love with it back when I was in college. Yes, it's easy enough for a college student "chef" to follow.

Ingredients

GF 

If soaking dry beans, start with 1 ¾ cups before soaking.

1 Tbs. olive oil, butter, ghee or coconut oil
1 medium onion, chopped
1 jalapeno pepper, seeded and chopped, optional
2 minced garlic cloves
4 c. chicken broth
2 cans great northern beans, drained and rinsed, OR about 4 c. cooked beans
2 Tbs. minced fresh parsley (or a scant Tbs. dried)
1 Tbs. lime juice
1 ½ tsp. ground cumin
2 Tbs. corn starch or arrowroot
¼ c. cold water
2 c. shredded cooked chicken
salt to taste, at least 1 tsp. if you use homemade chicken stock

Method

In a large saucepan, cook onion and pepper in oil over medium heat until tender, adding garlic for the last minute. Stir in broth, beans, parsley, lime juice and cumin – bring to a boil. Reduce heat, cover and simmer 10 minutes, stirring occasionally. Combine starch and water in a separate bowl or jar and mix or shake until smooth; stir into chili. Add chicken. Bring to a boil, cook and stir over medium heat for 2 minutes or until thickened slightly. Add salt and more cumin if necessary.

Serves at least 4.

Timesaver: This a super quick meal to begin with! Freeze your cooked chicken from making stock in 2-cup portions for an extra head start.

Substitutions and Frugal Tips

- ✓ *Substitution ideas:* You can switch out the spicy pepper for sweet bell peppers if you like.

- ✓ *Frugal tip:* Buy limes on sale (or better yet, reduced produce) and juice them all, freezing in 1 Tbs. portions in ice cube trays. Store in a bag in the freezer, and you can just throw one in the soup for fresh lime juice instead of bottled. (But that works too!)

FAQs

- ✓ It's freezer friendly!

Recipe adapted from the September/October 2000 edition of Quick Cooking *magazine.*

Cheesy White Chicken Chili

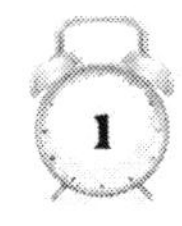      

Work Intensity Kid-Friendly Cost

This is a bit of a reverse engineered version of a 5 ingredient, throw it all in a slow cooker and walk away sort of meal. It tastes even better...but I included the quickie too!

Ingredients GF

If soaking dry beans, start with 1 ¾ cups before soaking.

1-2 Tbs. oil, extra virgin olive or coconut
1 medium onion, chopped
1 green pepper, chopped
1 jalapeno pepper, chopped
3 cloves garlic, minced
1 tsp. cumin
½ tsp. chili powder
½ tsp. oregano
½ tsp salt
2 c. cooked, shredded chicken
2 cans white beans, drained and rinsed, or 4 c. cooked beans
2 c. chicken stock or broth
1 pint (15 oz. can) diced tomatoes with juice
8 oz. Monterey Jack cheese, cubed or shredded

Method

In a soup pot, saute the onion, green pepper and jalapeno in oil (over medium-low heat if using EVOO) until limp. Add the minced garlic and saute another minute, then add the four spices and stir for a minute. Add the other ingredients *except* the cheese and cook until heated through. Stir prepared cheese into the soup, continuing to stir until melted over low heat or with heat off. Serve immediately.

Serves 4-6.

Timesaver: If you're in a big old hurry, try this version: 1 16 oz. jar salsa + 2 c. cooked chicken + 2 cans or one big jar white beans, drained and rinsed + 1 can chicken broth (no MSG) + 8 oz. Monterey Jack cheese, cubed. *Mix, heat, and serve!*

Substitutions and Frugal Tips

- ✓ *Substitution ideas:* Try pepperjack cheese for the super spicy version!
- ✓ Red or other colored peppers would be excellent.

FAQs

- ✓ Of course it's freezer friendly!

Black-Eyed Pea Soup

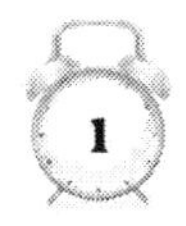

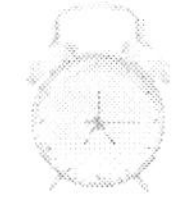
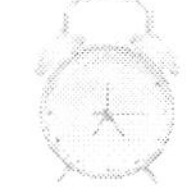
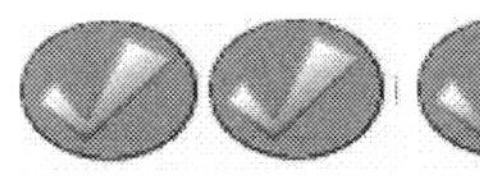

Work Intensity Kid-Friendly Cost

I'd never used black-eyed peas before preparing for this book, and I thought I should branch out. You know what? They're delightful!

Ingredients  

If soaking dry beans, start with 2 cups before soaking.

4 pieces of bacon
1 green pepper, chopped
1 medium onion, chopped
2-3 cloves garlic, minced
2 undrained cans of black eyed peas, or about 4 c. cooked black eyed peas
plus ½ c. cooking water
2 15-oz. cans of diced tomatoes, undrained (or 1 quart)
1-2 c. water, chicken or turkey stock, or bean cooking liquid
1 tsp. ground cumin
1 tsp. chili powder
1 tsp. ground mustard
1 tsp. salt
¼ tsp. pepper
shredded cheese (I prefer sharp cheddar)

Method

In a medium soup pot, cook the bacon and remove from the pot. Crumble and reserve for the table. Drain off all but about 1 Tbs. of bacon drippings and saute the green pepper and onion for 5-10 minutes until limp, adding the garlic at the end. Saute for another minute, then add the black eyed peas, tomatoes, water, and all the seasonings. Bring to a boil. Reduce heat and cover to simmer for 15-20 minutes.

Sprinkle with shredded cheese and cooked bacon to serve.

Yields 2 quarts and about 4-6 servings.

Timesaver: I always cook up a whole pound of bacon and simply freeze any leftovers. If you've got some frozen, this meal is 25% easier! You can substitute butter, olive oil, or tallow to saute the veggies if you don't keep your grease.

Substitutions and Frugal Tips

- ✓ *Substitution ideas:* You can switch green peppers for colored or double the peppers easily.
- ✓ *Italian variation:* Omit the mustard, chili powder, and cumin and use 1-2 tsp. of oregano or Italian seasoning instead. Top with croutons and mozzarella cheese.

FAQs

- ✓ *Can it be done without the bacon?* I suppose, but the bacon is the best part with the shredded cheese a close second. You may even want to have a few extra pieces on hand. You can also just incorporate the bacon right into the soup instead of serving it on the side, which makes leftovers a little less complicated.
- ✓ Freezer friendly!

Used with permission from Phoebe Hendricks of Getting Freedom From Debt (http://bit.ly/MRpOMp).

Simple Cabbage Soup with Secret Super Food

I created this one on the fly by combining two or three recipes by memory. It was one of my first times ever using cabbage, so I was just tickled when it turned out awesome, and totally unique! Your guests will never guess the hidden vegetable.

Ingredients GF CF

If soaking dry beans, start with 1-1 ½ cups before soaking.

2 Tbs. each olive oil and butter
1 large onion, coarsely chopped
3-5 stalks celery, sliced
3 carrots, sliced
4 cloves garlic, chopped
1-2 cans great northern or garbanzos, drained and rinsed, OR 2-4 c. cooked
1 tsp. salt
½ tsp. pepper
1+ tsp. cumin
½ head cabbage, thinly sliced
6 c. chicken stock
1-2 c. pumpkin
optional: 8 oz. can tomato sauce

Method

Melt butter and warm olive oil in a *large* soup pot. Add the onion, celery, carrots, garlic, and beans in order as you chop them. By the time you add the beans, the onions should be soft. Add salt, pepper, cumin and stir. Add cabbage and cover 5 minutes or so over medium-low heat to wilt. Pour in broth, pumpkin (frozen is fine) and optional tomato sauce. Bring to a boil, then reduce to a low simmer. Cover and cook 15-30 minutes until carrots and cabbage are tender.

Serves 6-10

Added Bonus: This soup has EIGHT super foods (http://www.kitchenstewardship.com/SuperFoods) and costs less than $3 for the whole batch if you play your seasonal cards right. Amazing!

Substitutions and Frugal Tips

- ✓ *Substitution ideas:* The tomato sauce is optional because our family liked the pumpkin-only version the best, but many people expect tomato with cabbage in a soup.

- ✓ You can use summer squash, pureed or not, or any fall squash in place of the pumpkin as well. Try turmeric as an interesting spice addition.

- ✓ *Frugal Tip:* Once you open a can of pumpkin for any recipe, freeze the rest immediately either in 1-cup portions or in ice cube trays for ease of use later. Frozen pumpkin works fine in muffin and bread recipes once thawed.

- ✓ *Frugal Tip:* Buy cabbage when it's in season (fall at the Farmer's Market and around St. Patrick's Day in the grocery store) for super cheap and then shred, lightly steam and freeze in plastic bags for this recipe or others with cooked cabbage.

- ✓ Did you know you could also freeze celery (http://www.kitchenstewardship.com/FreezerPrep)? Never let another half bag of the stuff go to waste!

FAQs

- ✓ *What to do with the rest of the pumpkin?*
  - ✓ Pumpkin muffins: http://www.kitchenstewardship.com/OneBowlPumpkin
  - ✓ Pumpkin cookies: http://www.kitchenstewardship.com/PumpkinCookies
  - ✓ Deal with leftover pumpkin: http://www.kitchenstewardship.com/Pumpkin20Ways

- ✓ *What to do with the rest of the cabbage?*
  - ✓ Beef and Cabbage Pockets: http://bit.ly/1iXvqiR
  - ✓ Cabbage Salad with Goat Cheese: http://www.kitchenstewardship.com/CabbageSalad
  - ✓ You can also just use it in a salad or a stir fry at random.

- ✓ Soup always freezes well.

- ✓ See the original with cost breakdown and anecdotes here: http://www.kitchenstewardship.com/SimpleCabbageSoup

Black Bean Soup

Work Intensity Kid-Friendly Cost

A simple, vegetable-laden, meatless or chicken stock based soup that we could eat once a week. Some of the beans and veggies are pureed, so it's kid-friendly to boot.

Ingredients

GF CF If soaking dry beans, start with 3 cups before soaking.

1-2 Tbs. oil (extra virgin olive or coconut oil)
1 onion, chopped
1 red pepper, chopped
1 jalapeno, chopped (to taste)
2-3 cloves minced garlic
3 carrots, chopped or sliced
1-2 tsp. chili powder
2 tsp.-1 Tbs. ground cumin
4 c. homemade chicken stock *(or use the "broth" from cooking dry beans, with or without adding extra veggies for flavor)*
3 cans black beans, drained and rinsed, OR ~6 c. cooked beans
1 15-oz. can (or home canned pint) diced or whole tomatoes
1 c. frozen corn (optional)
1/4 tsp. ground pepper
1/2 tsp. salt, if using unsalted broth

Method

In a large pot, heat oil over medium and cook onion and peppers for a few minutes until soft. Add garlic, carrots, and all spices and cook and stir for one minute.

Pour in the broth, 2 cups (or 1 can) of beans, corn and pepper. Bring to a boil.

The can of tomatoes and remaining beans need to be pureed before adding to the pot. I like to do this in the can or jar with my stick blender when possible, but a food processor or blender works well too. Add to the pot, and once everything is boiling, reduce the heat to low. Cover and simmer for 10-15 minutes until the carrots are tender.

Serves at least 6. Easy to double!

Serving options: Serve with a dollop of sour cream or guacamole on top and some shredded cheese to pass at the table.

Our favorite side for this Mexi-style soup is cheese quesadillas on homemade whole wheat tortillas (http://www.kitchenstewardship.com/WWTortilla). They make the best dippers!

Crunchy tortillas chips or corn muffins also go perfectly next to the black bean soup and may be a good bribe to get kids or husbands to finish their bowls.

Substitutions and Frugal Tips

- ✓ *Substitution ideas:* A reviewer reports that it's still tasty without any of the peppers. You can always switch out one sort of pepper for another, too.
- ✓ *Even more kid-friendly option:* Add 2/3 of the beans to the pot along with the tomatoes, then blend everything right in the pot with a stick blender. Add the final two cups of beans whole. The resulting soup is not as appetizing to look at, but the taste is the same and more vegetables are pureed, so more may get past the kid-meter.
- ✓ *Frugal tip:* Buy jalapenos by the quart in the summer locally, and chop and freeze them for simple soups throughout the winter. Peppers do not need to be blanched before freezing. Just remember that the seeds have the heat.

FAQs

- ✓ *What if I don't have an immersion blender?* Of course a larger blender will work fine, but if you don't want the hassle of another dirty dish, just leave everything whole.
- ✓ Very freezer friendly.

Recipe inspired by this one (http://bit.ly/1ns8GYL) from allrecipes.com and Rachael Ray's black bean soup.

Tuscan Bean Soup

 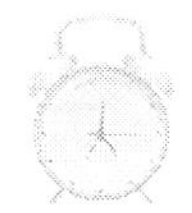      

Work Intensity Kid-Friendly Cost

This is a super simple soup in every way, both in flavor and work involved. A good dipping sandwich makes all the difference!

Ingredients

  If soaking dry beans, start with 3 cups before soaking.

2 Tbs. olive oil
1 medium onion, diced
3 garlic cloves, minced
1 tsp. thyme
1 tsp. oregano
¼ tsp. rosemary or marjoram
4 c. chicken stock
3 cans white (great northern) beans, drained and rinsed
OR about 5-6 c. cooked white beans, divided
1 tsp. salt (if using homemade stock, less if not)
5 oz. baby spinach

Method

Saute chopped onions in oil in a large pot over medium or medium-low heat, stirring occasionally to prevent browning. Put the cover on to speed up the softening if you like. After about 5-8 minutes when the onions are completely soft, add the garlic and herbs and cook 1-2 minutes more. (Sometimes I toss in both marjoram and rosemary if I'm feeling plucky.) The aroma will be delectable.

Stir in broth and 4 cups of the beans, increase heat to high, cover, and bring to a boil. Add salt to taste, reduce heat, and simmer 5-10 minutes.

Puree soup in the pot using a stick blender (immersion blender), or blend in 2-3 small batches in a blender. Return soup to the saucepan, add the remaining 2 cups beans and spinach, then heat to a simmer. Serve hot.

Serves 4-6.

Timesaver: If you're in a hurry, just use a stick blender to partially puree the soup in the pot without removing any beans. You'll still have some intact beans and save yourself 5 minutes and a few dirty dishes. I highly recommend a stick blender!

Added Bonus: The spinach will help your body assimilate the iron in the beans better.

Substitutions and Frugal Tips

- ✓ *Substitution ideas:*
    - You can use just about any green instead of spinach if you like.
    - Adding carrots is an easy step to get in more vegetables.
    - A pinch of cayenne may give this soup the kick you desire if it seems too bland for your family's tastes.
    - Add 1/2-1 cup cooked ground sausage or some crumbled bacon to take the soup to the next level.

- ✓ For a little more flavor, you can also sauté the onions even longer, until lightly browned, before adding the garlic.

- ✓ *Grow it up:* Deglaze the pot with 1/4 cup of dry white wine after browning the onions.

FAQs

- ✓ *Can I make it totally meatless?* Yes. The recipe works out just fine with the vegetable broth/bean broth method on p. 18. It's a perfect simple meal for a Lenten Friday, in my opinion.

- ✓ *What do you dip?* This is a great soup for dipping sandwiches — grilled cheese is good, grilled mozzarella cheese with sauteed sliced mushrooms and red onions even better!

- ✓ *What do I do with the rest of the bag of spinach?* You can lightly steam spinach and freeze it in ice cube trays for green smoothies (http://www.kitchenstewardship.com/GreenSmoothies), or plan another meal for the week to use up the bag. Some of our favorites include:
    *Sausage, Bean and Greens Soup (p. 37)
    *Beef and Bean Stew a la Tuscany (p. 75)
    *Sausage Spinach Pasta Toss (http://www.kitchenstewardship.com/SausagePastaToss)
    *In scrambled eggs (http://www.kitchenstewardship.com/ScrambledEggs)
    *Sneak into many other soups, casseroles, or wraps
    *Ways to stash spinach: http://www.kitchenstewardship.com/MMSpinach

- ✓ Freezes great!

Three Bean Soup

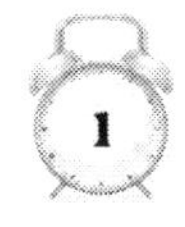

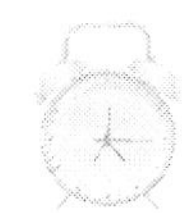
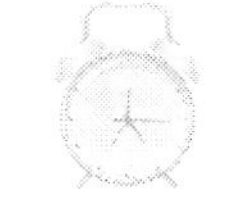

Work Intensity Kid-Friendly Cost

I'm always thankful for a simple meal and love to be able to turn to this recipe. It's often a hit with kids who don't love beans and can even transform into something else for leftovers the next day!

Ingredients

GF

If soaking dry beans, use 1 ½ c. white beans & ¾ c. each pintos and kidneys.

1 Tbs. oil
2 medium onions, chopped
1-2 cloves garlic, crushed
salt and pepper to taste
1/2-2 tsp. chili powder
1/2-2 tsp. cumin
1-2 tsp. dried thyme
2 15-oz cans great northern beans, drained and rinsed OR 4 c. cooked beans
1 15-oz can kidney beans, drained and rinsed OR 2 c. cooked
1 15-oz can pinto beans, drained and rinsed OR 2 c. cooked
4 c. chicken stock or vegetable broth (see p. 18)
¾ c. grated cheddar cheese
¼ c. finely chopped green onions, optional
1 tsp. salt (if using homemade broth)

Method

In a large pot, heat oil over medium heat. Add onions and cook 5-10 minutes, stirring occasionally, until limp or even browned, depending on your taste. Stir in garlic, salt, pepper, chili powder, cumin and thyme; cook 1 minute. Add beans, stir well, and cook 1 minute.

Raise heat to high; add the broth. Bring to a boil, reduce heat to low, cover, and let cook 10 minutes. Working in batches, puree the soup in a food processor, blender, or in the pot with an immersion blender (much faster!) until smooth and thick. You can also leave part of the beans whole for a pretty multi-colored look.

Simmer over low heat for a few minutes. Season to taste. Serve hot, sprinkled with grated cheese and green onions. We like to pair with a simple grilled cheese for dipping. Tortilla chips are also excellent.

Serves 6-8

Substitutions and Frugal Tips

- ✓ *Substitution ideas:* You can switch out some of the beans for other varieties of beans if you're running low on anything.
- ✓ *Recipe conversion:* Just boil down a little to thicken it up, and you've got refried beans for quesadillas or nachos the next day at lunch!

FAQs

- ✓ *How spicy? ½ to 2 teaspoons is quite a range.* If your kiddos can handle some spice, I'd highly recommend 2 teaspoons of each spice. Cut back on the chili powder first, then the cumin, if anyone in your family doesn't like spicy foods. You'll likely find that you need at least a teaspoon of salt. If it tastes bland but you're not a "spicy" lover, add more salt first.
- ✓ Freezer friendly!

This recipe was originally listed as a "kid-friendly" recipe in Parents *magazine.*

Homemade Limey Refried Beans

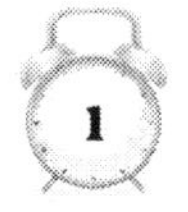

Work Intensity Kid-Friendly Cost

There are probably a million ways to make homemade refried beans, all of them healthier than a can. You could just mash pintos with oil and salt, add some heat if you like them spicy, or take a unique twist like this one.

Ingredients GF

If soaking dry beans, start with 1 ½ cups before soaking.

- 3 ½ c. cooked pinto, kidney or black beans
- 2 Tbs. olive oil or lard
- 1 c. finely chopped onions
- 1 tsp. whole cumin seeds or ½ tsp. ground cumin
- 1-3 large cloves garlic, minced
- ½ tsp. dried oregano or Mexican oregano
- ½-1 tsp. salt
- ½ c. grated jalapeno jack cheese
- ½ to 3 Tbs. freshly squeezed lime juice
- ¼ to ½ tsp. grated lime zest (optional)

Method

When you drain your beans, *reserve the cooking liquid* to thin the refried beans.

In the pot from the cooked beans, heat the oil. Add the onions and cumin and cook over medium heat, stirring occasionally, until the onions are limp, about 5 minutes. Add the garlic and oregano and cook, stirring frequently, until onions are lightly browned, 2-3 minutes more.

Stir in 1 cup of the bean cooking liquid and add half the beans. Use a potato masher to mash them. Add remaining beans and mash. Better yet, remove from the heat temporarily and use a stick blender. You can leave the mixture quite uneven with some beans intact, or continue mashing until fairly smooth. Stir well and make sure the beans are thoroughly heated. Use medium heat or lower unless you are nearby and can stir often over higher heat.

When most of the liquid has been absorbed, turn off the heat. Stir in the cheese, lime juice, lime zest, and salt to taste. Use in any recipe that calls for refried beans or serve as a side with Mexican food.

Makes about 4-5 cups, or 2-3 cans worth.

Timesaver: I double this recipe almost every single time. The refried beans freeze just fine, either in 1-cup or 2-cup portions for meals or even in ice cube trays for the occasional quick quesadillas when you just need a little.

Added Bonus: It's pretty fun to play with this recipe – leave out the cheese for a dairy free and *much* more frugal alternative, play with the different beans (black beans are my new favorite "refried" version), and omit the lime juice and experiment with various spices, adding heat as you wish.

Substitutions and Frugal Tips

- ✓ *Substitution ideas:* You can switch out the jalapeno jack cheese for sharp cheddar or even feta for a more sophisticated version.
- ✓ Serve with pumpkin seeds or radish slices to be authentically Mexican.
- ✓ Simply add a teaspoon of chili powder without changing a thing for a nice spicy overtone.
- ✓ Add ½ cup thinly sliced green onions when you add the cheese.

FAQs

- ✓ *Why don't you give the amount of beans in cans?* Really, if you're going to start with cans, you might as well grab a can of fat-free refried beans and add your own fat.
- ✓ *Can I use these beans cold in a dip or appetizer dish?* They work just fine. In fact, check out the next recipe for our family's favorite tortilla chip dipping spread.
- ✓ *They taste bland. What's going on?* Most likely, you need to add more salt. That often happens to me since I don't salt my beans while they cook. Either that, or your family really needs the extra spices. Play around and make it work for you!

Recipe adapted from Pressure Perfect.

7-Layer Tex Mex Appetizer Dip

Work Intensity Kid-Friendly Cost

People cannot stop eating this dip, and even my small children have been known to finish off nearly half the tray by themselves. A way to win friends at parties.

Ingredients GF

About 2 c. homemade refried beans, previous recipe
Homemade guacamole, recipe here: http://bit.ly/eYWZz9
¾ c. homemade mayo, recipe here: http://bit.ly/cqNGkb
¾ c. sour cream
2 Tbs. or one packet taco seasoning
Shredded cheese, usually about one 8-oz. package or 2 cups
Sliced black olives
Chopped tomatoes
Sliced green onions

Method

Be sure to have chilled refried beans on hand and make the homemade guacamole fresh. In a separate bowl, stir together the mayonnaise, sour cream and taco seasoning. Choose a 9x13 glass dish or small cookie sheet (13x10" is perfect, although you can stretch it to fit a standard 15x10"), taking into consideration how you'll cover it to store in the refrigerator.

Layer the ingredients in order listed, starting with the refried beans, guacamole and taco seasoned mixture. Use a spatula to spread evenly. Make the top pretty with the cheese, olives, tomatoes, and onions.

Store cold and serve within a day for best quality, although the dip will be acceptable as leftovers for a couple days. Pair with tortilla chips or veggies for dipping.

Serves...? How hungry are your guests?

Added Bonus: Seasonal decorative trays are often an excellent size as well and perfect for parties.

Substitutions and Frugal Tips

- ✓ *Substitution ideas:* Once the bottom 3 layers are in place, you can leave out pretty much anything and it's still an excellent dip. When tomatoes aren't in season, I skip them every time. I don't really love black olives and rarely think ahead enough to buy green onions, so we typically serve this as a 4-layer dip. It's the sour cream/taco seasoning layer that is the key to success, if you want to know our family's humble opinion. Addicting, even without MSGs!

- ✓ Be sure to watch for avocados on sale, often during the wintertime in the States. They are ripe and ready to cut when there is just the slightest bit of give to the skin; once they actually "squish" they're generally a bit overripe and just don't taste as good. Ripen on the counter, and you can store an avocado in the refrigerator for up to a week once it's ready to eat.

- ✓ I highly recommend purchasing quality extra virgin olive oil in bulk for making homemade mayo and salad dressings.

FAQs

- ✓ *What's your recipe for homemade taco seasoning?* I use Amy's, right here: http://bit.ly/1bmgY4K Make about 5-10 times the recipe once you know you like it so you always have some on hand.

- ✓ *What do you do with extra green onions and black olives?* I do buy a larger can of black olives, since the price is often almost the same as a tiny can. Olives will freeze for soups just fine. Toss them into your chili for a neat twist. Green onions also can be frozen without blanching if used in cooked dishes. You can add some to your next batch of refried beans or scrambled eggs.

- ✓ *Can I freeze it?* No, unfortunately not. Guacamole and the creamy layer would not fare so well, nor would the veggies on top.

Mexican Beans and Rice

No need to buy a box for an easy side dish for taco night. For mere pennies, you can make a huge batch of beans and rice to suit any palate.

Ingredients GF CF

1 c. brown rice
1 ¾ c. water
8 oz. can tomato sauce (1 cup)
2 Tbs. taco seasoning
1 can kidney or black beans (~2 cups cooked dry beans)
usually needs salt, about ½ tsp. to taste

Method

Saute the rice first either in a dry pot or in a bit of butter (or both, one after the other). Keep stirring constantly over medium-high heat until brown. Notice this is *not black*. That transition happens quickly, so keep a close eye. *This* is the trick to really make it all taste and feel like a boxed mix, but you can skip it and still enjoy the dish if you're low on time (or forget). It will work whether you're soaking (see below) or not, and totally changes the mouthfeel and taste of the finished dish, definitely for the better.

Add the water, tomato sauce and taco seasoning. If it seems that a lot of water evaporated into steam when you added it to the hot pot, you might add an extra ¼ cup as insurance.

Bring to a boil, turn heat to low, and simmer covered for 40 minutes (no peeking!). At this point *almost* all the water should be absorbed, although you might notice that the tomato sauce has risen to the top. Just stir it in. Add the beans and optional add-ins and simmer 5 more minutes, covered, to finish cooking the rice. You might need a few extra minutes of cooking and stirring to get the beans heated through, adding a bit of water if you have a thin pot bottom or worry about scorching your rice.

Serves 4-8 adults; about twice as much as a standard boxed mix.

Timesaver: For me, adding chopped onions and peppers keeps it as easy as a box mix because they're always already prepped in my freezer (http://www.kitchenstewardship.com/FreezerPrep), frozen from the farmer's market for the winter!

Added Bonus: The sky is the limit on variations of this dish, from different beans to different add-ins to playing with the spices.

Substitutions and Frugal Tips

✓ *Optional add-ins:*

- 1 cup frozen corn
- chopped onion
- minced garlic
- chopped green peppers
- colored peppers
- chili peppers
- shredded cheese

Giving onions, peppers, or garlic a quick saute before adding will enhance the flavor and avoid the "bite" of fresh onions, for example. You might use another pan to accomplish this or simply saute in fat before adding the rice and leave the vegetables in the pot for the entire cooking time.

✓ *Substitution ideas:* You can switch out the taco seasoning for something milder like cumin and oregano, or experiment with seasoning blends like Southwest seasoning or ancho chili powder, for example.

✓ Try a can of diced tomatoes with green chiles (undrained, and omit ¼ c. more liquid) instead of the tomato sauce and put the beans on the side for a more "Spanish rice" flair.

✓ Don't be afraid to try a different bean if you don't have the right ones on hand!

✓ *Frugal tip:* This is definitely a recipe where you want to have frozen home-cooked beans on hand. It's really not worth the energy costs to soak and cook just 2 cups for 4-8 hours. Use a can if you're in a bind.

FAQs

- ✓ *What about the additives in taco seasoning packets?* For chemical-free taco seasoning, you can mix your own. I do it in bulk with this recipe: http://bit.ly/1bmgY4K
- ✓ *Can it freeze?* It does lose a little in quality, but ultimately the rice and beans freeze acceptably.

Healthy Upgrade: Soaked

Soak brown rice following this rice soaking method (http://www.kitchenstewardship.com/FermentedRice) overnight or for 7 hours. Drain and add water (minus about ¼ cup) and tomato sauce at cooking time and continue as usual.

If you're soaking, you can still saute the dry rice first, then add the liquid, and just soak at room temperature. It's also possible to soak the rice overnight, drain, and saute the wet, soaked rice in a bit of butter or oil. It takes considerably longer for the rice to brown because it has to dry out first (maybe about 10 minutes). Don't go far away because the browning will happen fast once it happens, but be patient.

Chicken Rice-a-Roni Substitute

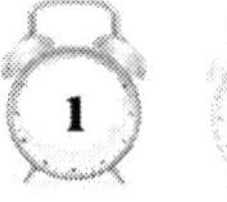

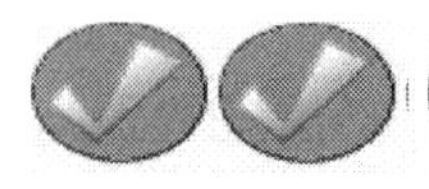

Work Intensity Kid-Friendly Cost

Our local Pampered Chef guru verbally mentioned this recipe, and it was so easy I could make it just from her one-minute spiel. You'll never need a box again!

Ingredients GF CF

1-2 Tbs. butter or olive oil
1 medium onion, chopped (about ½ cup)
1-2 stalks chopped celery
1-2 cloves garlic, minced (optional)
1 c. brown rice
2 c. chicken broth (½ cup less if soaking, see below)
1 15-oz. can of black, kidney, garbanzo or other beans, drained and rinsed, or 1 ½-2 c. cooked dry beans
salt and pepper to taste (usually at least 1 tsp. salt and ¼ tsp. pepper)

Method

In a 2-quart or larger pot with a lid, saute onion and celery in a little water, oil or butter 5 minutes until limp, stirring occasionally. Add the garlic for the last minute of sauteing. Add chicken broth and rice, salt and pepper; bring to a boil. Reduce heat to low, cover and simmer 40 minutes until rice is cooked and liquid is almost absorbed. No peeking, no stirring allowed until the time is up!

Quickly add the beans to the rice and cook on low, covered, for another 5 minutes. The rice should be sufficiently cooked, but you may need to cook and stir for a few more minutes to heat the beans all the way through. If the liquid isn't completely absorbed, cook a bit longer until the rice is absolutely tender.

Tip: To get the "real" rice-a-roni texture: before beginning the process, saute the rice in butter over medium-high heat, stirring constantly for a few minutes until rice is just browning. With this method, you may have to saute the onions and celery in a separate pan (so the rice doesn't get overbrowned), so you have to be willing to do the extra dishes. If you have a boxed mix loving family to please, though, it's worth the extra step to be authentic.

Serves 4-6 adults.

Timesaver: If you have celery and onion chopped in your freezer (http://www.kitchenstewardship.com/FreezerPrep), this is just as quick as the boxed stuff!

Added Bonus: It only costs about $1 with homemade chicken stock (http://www.kitchenstewardship.com/MakeStock); $1.50-2 if using canned, but it makes a MUCH bigger batch than the little boxes of Rice-a-Roni, and the nutrition is far superior because you're using brown rice and healthy fats, plus no MSGs.

Substitutions and Frugal Tips

- ✓ *Substitution ideas:* Feel free to use just about any bean in this recipe, switch out the celery for sweet peppers, and add spices (cayenne pepper, simple marjoram, and use your imagination) or spicy peppers to zoop it up a little!
- ✓ *Tip*: If you don't have homemade stock, one 14.5-oz. can of broth plus a little water makes two cups.

FAQs

- ✓ *Why don't you include soaked dry bean amounts?* For this small amount, it's really not worth it to dirty a pot and turn on your stove. Either use frozen home-cooked beans or a can.
- ✓ *Does it freeze?* This recipe freezes acceptably in single serving sizes.

Healthy Upgrade: Soaked

Soak brown rice in 2 cups water following this rice soaking method (http://www.kitchenstewardship.com/FermentedRice) for 7-12 hours or overnight. Drain and add 1 1/2 cups chicken broth (no water) when it's time to cook. (The rice soaks up ½ cup of water in the soaking process.)

If you're soaking, you can still saute the dry rice first for the box mix texture, then add the liquid, and just soak at room temperature. It's also possible to soak the rice overnight, drain, and saute the wet, soaked rice in a bit of butter or oil. It takes considerably longer for the rice to brown because it has to dry out first (maybe about 10 minutes). Don't go far away because the browning will happen fast once it happens, but be patient.

Cuban Black Beans and Rice

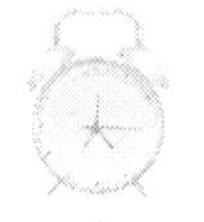

Work Intensity Kid-Friendly Cost

This recipe (there are really two of them) came about as I tried to reverse engineer Vigo brand Cuban black beans and rice, melding together about 4 recipes into one.

Ingredients

GF  If soaking dry beans, start with 1-1 ½ cups before soaking.

4 slices bacon
2-4 Tbs. olive oil, butter, ghee, or bacon fat
1 c. brown rice

1 large onion, chopped
1/2-1 green pepper, chopped
1 jalapeno pepper, chopped
4 cloves minced garlic

2-3 tsp. cumin
1 Tbs. dried parsley
1 tsp. pepper
dash cayenne, to taste
bay leaf
1 tsp. oregano
1 tsp. salt
2-3 c. cooked black beans
1 8 oz. can tomato sauce (1 cup)
1/4 c. red wine
1 1/2 c. water or bean cooking liquid
2 Tbs. red wine vinegar

Method

In a medium saucepan (at least 3 quarts), cook 4 slices of bacon until crisp. Remove to a plate. Then in the bacon fat or an additional 2-4 tablespoons of fat, sauté the onions, peppers, and brown rice until the rice is just barely beginning to brown and the vegetables are limp. Add garlic for the last minute.

Stir in the 7 spices, from cumin to salt, and the black beans; stir and cook one minute. Add the cooked and crumbled bacon, tomato sauce, wine and water. Bring to a boil and simmer on low with the lid on for 30 minutes. Add red wine vinegar and simmer, covered, 15 more minutes or until rice is tender.

Serves 6-8 adults.

Timesaver: Keep already cooked and crumbled bacon in the freezer for recipes like this. You can start 20 minutes into the recipe if you've got that handy.

Added Bonus: Here's another recipe version! I prefer the one above, but this one is also delicious and goes over already cooked rice.

Cuban Black Beans Over Rice

Ingredients:

2 c. dry black beans, soaked and cooked, OR 4 c. black beans; reserve some bean cooking liquid

1/3-2/3 c. olive oil
1 large onion, chopped
1 green pepper, chopped (or other colors will do as well)
4 cloves garlic, minced
1 bay leaf
1-2 tsp. oregano
2+ tsp. cumin
pinch cayenne (to taste)
1 tsp. pepper
scant Tbs. salt
2 Tbs. sugar
1/2 c. red wine
2 Tbs. red wine vinegar
cooked brown rice

Method:

In a large pot, saute the onion and pepper in oil until nicely browned, adding the garlic for the last minute, then add the seven seasonings and stir for a minute or two. Add the beans, wine and up to 1 cup bean cooking liquid. Bring to a boil, reduce heat and simmer uncovered for half an hour, then add 2 Tbs. red wine vinegar and cook 15 minutes longer. Serve over cooked brown rice.

Substitutions and Frugal Tips

✓ *Substitution ideas:* Both dishes are pretty versatile...
- ✓ You can leave out the peppers entirely.
- ✓ Feel free to use dried minced onion and garlic instead of fresh.
- ✓ Leave out the sugar or sub a few drops liquid stevia.
- ✓ White vinegar can replace red wine vinegar if you don't have it on hand.

✓ *Quick tip:* For the second recipe, your prep can be really speedy if you already have cooked brown rice on hand. I recommend making stir fry or the Black-Eyed Pea Casserole recipe from p. 85 and doubling or tripling your batch of rice. If you have leftovers, you can freeze cooked brown rice in ½-cup servings for easy leftovers or stir fry night later.

✓ *Frugal tip:* Any time you have a smidge of leftover wine in a bottle, freeze it in ice cube trays and use in cooking recipes.

FAQs

- ✓ *Can I make it less spicy?* Simple. Just leave out the jalapeno and reduce the cumin to a scant 2 teaspoons. The dish will still have plenty of flavor.
- ✓ *Kosher?* Skip the bacon or simply use the second recipe.
- ✓ *Gluten-free?* Just leave out the red wine vinegar or replace with apple cider vinegar, half as much.
- ✓ *I don't have tomato sauce on hand; what do I do?* You can easily substitute a 6-oz. can of tomato paste and add another ¼ cup water to the recipe.
- ✓ *I don't cook with wine; what can I do?* Just use an equal amount of broth (vegetable or chicken) or water plus (optional) ½ tsp. Bragg's liquid aminos.
- ✓ *I have a lot left...*It goes great in a wrap as well as a side dish for many different kinds of meals.
- ✓ *Does it freeze well?* Acceptably, but not great. I would try to use it within the week if possible.

Healthy Upgrade: Soaked

To soak the rice for the first version, start like this:

In a medium saucepan (at least 3 quarts), saute brown rice in the fat until barely browned, then add enough water to cover plus water from the accelerated fermentation method (http://www.kitchenstewardship.com/FermentedRice). After soaking at room temperature for 7-24 hours, drain the rice completely in a colander (one that won't let all your rice go right through).

Once the pot is empty, cook the bacon and proceed with the directions starting with the sauteed vegetables. Add the soaked rice back in with the cooked bacon.

Pasta with White (Bean) Sauce

If you don't tell your dinner guests you're serving beans, they'll be hard-pressed to figure out the difference between this protein-packed white sauce and a standard Alfredo. You can choose to leave the beans whole for a lovely texture, too.

Ingredients GF

If soaking dry beans, start with 1 cup before soaking.

- 2 Tbs. butter
- ½ c. chopped onion
- 1 4-oz. can diced green chili peppers, drained, or 1 chopped jalapeno or Anaheim pepper
- 2 cloves garlic, minced
- 2 Tbs. whole wheat flour or arrowroot starch*
- 1/8-1/4 tsp. black pepper
- 1 ½ c. whole milk
- 1 ½ c. shredded cheese (any kind works, but Swiss or Monterey Jack is great)
- 1 15-oz. can white beans, drained and rinsed, OR 2 c. cooked dry beans
- salt to taste, likely about a ½ tsp.
- ½ lb. Linguine or favorite pasta, cooked according to package directions

Method

In a medium-sized, heavy bottomed pot, cook onion and peppers (if using fresh) in melted butter until tender, adding garlic at the last minute. Stir in flour and pepper and cook two minutes. Add the milk all at once. *(*GF version with arrowroot: Follow directions for butter, onion, peppers, then add 1 c. milk. Bring to a boil. Mix arrowroot with the remaining 1/2 cup milk. Stir into boiling liquid.)*

Cook and stir over medium heat until bubbly and thickened, taking care not to scorch the bottom. Cook one more minute, then add cheese and stir to melt. Add the beans and canned chiles (if using canned) and stir to heat through. Feel free to add extra milk at any point if the sauce is too thick for your tastes. Serve over linguine or your favorite pasta. You might include steamed veggies right in the sauce for an all-in-one meal.

For the bean haters of the world: If you use an immersion blender and whiz the sauce, the beans (and their taste) disappear. You might want to add a bit of extra milk to thin it out, up to 1/4-1/2 cup.

Serves 4.

Timesaver: Balance your steamer basket over the pasta water for the last 5 minutes or so of the cooking time and your steamed veggies will be done in one pot and at the same time as your pasta for a super easy meal.

Substitutions and Frugal Tips

- ✓ *Substitution ideas:* Adding some diced red pepper in the saute or any vegetable you might include in a stir fry, whether right in the sauce or just stirred in with the sauce and pasta, creates some delicious new options.

- ✓ *Add meat:* Grilled chicken on top takes the pasta right up to restaurant quality. It can be a complete meatless meal in itself, or it can serve as a healthy side dish.

- ✓ *Go grain-free:* Use spaghetti squash underneath the sauce for a higher veggie count, lower carbs and no grains/gluten.

- ✓ *Frugal tips:* Buy jalapeno (and other kinds of) peppers at the Farmer's Market or the reduced produce section at your grocery store. Peppers can be chopped and frozen without blanching or any other treatments. It's easy to grab a handful of chopped peppers from a bag in the freezer and toss them right into the saute pot. You can also use a less expensive cheese of any kind.

- ✓ *Something fun to try:* Use the sauce as a base for a pizza!

FAQs

- ✓ *How is this meal gluten-free?* The sauce works great with gluten-free pasta.

- ✓ *Does it have to be a compromise meal?* You can, of course, make your own pasta, which launches the dish from a "compromise quick meal" to a traditional foods healthy option, or just used cooked brown rice.

- ✓ *Freezer friendly?* Pasta really doesn't freeze well, but the sauce should fare acceptably in the freezer. Thin with milk to reheat.

Pesto "Bean"-fredo with Chicken

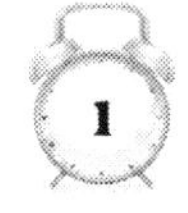

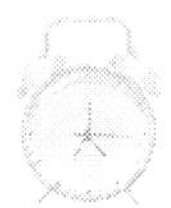
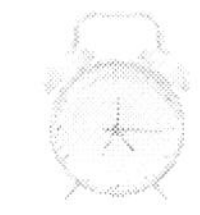
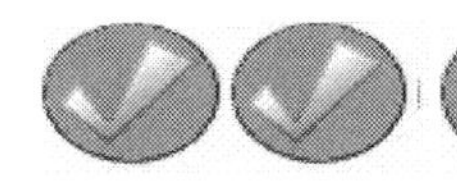

Work Intensity Kid-Friendly Cost

You just might try licking the immersion blender after making this sauce like one reviewer and her daughter. Just be sure to unplug it first!

Ingredients GF

1/3 pound pasta, any kind
about 2 c. broccoli florets
2 Tbs. olive oil
½ red pepper, chopped
1 ½ c. cooked white beans or one can, drained and rinsed
¼ c. shredded Parmesan cheese
¼ c. whole milk
1-2 Tbs. pesto
a few thick slices or about 1/2 c. shredded mozzarella cheese
½ tsp. salt
10 grinds black pepper
optional: spinach
grilled chicken

Method

Cook pasta as directed and add broccoli (and even chopped stems) to the water the last 5 minutes. If you balance your steamer basket on top of the pasta, all the better so you don't lose so many nutrients in the water. Drain into a colander and allow to sit and wait.

In the same pot, sauté the red pepper in olive oil over medium heat for a few minutes. Add beans, Parmesan, milk and pesto. Blend well with an immersion blender. (You could transfer to a traditional blender or food processor if you don't have an immersion blender.) Add the mozzarella, salt and pepper and heat through on low, stirring occasionally, until the cheese is melted. Add up to ¼ cup more milk to reach desired consistency, as it is usually a rather thick paste at this point. Return the pasta and broccoli to the pot, adding a few handfuls of spinach if you have some on hand. Mix well and heat through. Really makes a meal with grilled chicken on top!

Makes 4 small servings.

Added Bonus: A double batch of this sauce works great for a ½ pound of pasta, which easily feeds a family of four with some leftovers. Just think – two cans of beans in a regular old pasta meal, and no one has to know!

Substitutions and Frugal Tips

- ✓ *Substitution ideas*: 2 Tbs. fresh basil or 2 tsp. dried basil would substitute for the pesto in a pinch, since you're already using olive oil and Parmesan, the other main ingredients in a pesto.

- ✓ *Frugal tip:* Make homemade pesto in the summer when fresh basil is abundant and freeze in 1 Tbs. sized "plops" on waxed paper on a cookie sheet. Store in a freezer bag for use all through the winter! One "plop" seasons this recipe just perfectly.

- ✓ *Homemade pesto recipe*: 4 garlic cloves, 1/4 c. Parmesan cheese, 1/4 c. walnuts, 2 c. packed basil leaves, 1 Tbs. lemon juice, 1/4 c. extra virgin olive oil. Chop garlic in a food processor; whiz chunk of Parmesan if needed. Nuts next, then basil. Stream in lemon juice and olive oil while running the processor. *Makes about 1 c. pesto.*

Spaghetti and Pinto Bean Chili

You may be surprised how much you enjoy this twist on two traditional comfort foods.

Ingredients GF CF

1 Tbs. oil
1 medium onion, chopped
2 cans green chiles or equivalent chopped fresh peppers (see notes)
1 tsp. cumin
1 Tbs. chili powder
1 Tbs. taco seasoning or ½ packet
2 15-oz. cans diced tomatoes with juice or 1 qt. home canned
2-3 c. water or stock
1/4-1/3 lb. uncooked spaghetti, broken ~4 times or into 1" pieces for children
1 can pinto beans, drained and rinsed, OR 2 c. cooked pintos

Method

In a large pot, saute the onions and chiles or peppers in oil for about 5 minutes. Add spices and stir to combine for a minute, then add tomatoes and water. Bring to a boil. Stir in broken spaghetti, bring to a boil again and simmer, uncovered, for 10 minutes. Add the beans and simmer 5 more minutes until heated through. Serve hot with optional shredded cheese.

Serves 4 adults with no leftovers

Timesaver: This is a good recipe for which to have frozen pintos on hand, and my frozen peppers save lots of time and money.

Added Bonus: It doubles so easily for simple leftovers!

Substitutions and Frugal Tips

- ✓ *Substitution ideas*: For a frugal and whole foods alternative to canned chiles, dice 1 jalapeno, seeded, OR ½ Anaheim pepper, OR ½ poblano. Consider your family's tastes when adding the heat!
- ✓ *Add vegetables:* Half of a green or red bell pepper, a diced or shredded zucchini, or fresh greens all fit well into this dish, even all three at once.
- ✓ *Less spicy:* This recipe is definitely too spicy for many children, so if your family is a "mild" sort, cut the chili powder and taco seasoning in half, at least, or omit the spicy peppers entirely. Taste and add more taco seasoning if needed.
- ✓ *Want to use a different bean?* Why not! Black or kidney would be wonderful.
- ✓ *Gluten-free no-pasta adaptation:* Gluten-free pasta works fine, but it's expensive. You can substitute 1 c. dry quinoa, soaked in water overnight, for the spaghetti noodles. Just simmer for 35 minutes instead of 10 after adding the quinoa and getting back to a boil, and only use 2 cups of water or stock. You'll get a nice, thick chili that's begging for extra vegetables to be added.

FAQs

- ✓ *Really, how much water should I use?* If you hate having to guess between 2 and 3 cups, this will help: Using all 3 cups water makes for a soupy chili, and you can't really drain off the water at the end because a lot of the spices rest there. If you like a thicker, heartier chili or a result more like a hamburger helper recipe where most or all of the liquid ends up absorbed, I recommend using only 2 cups water. You can always sneak a little bit in or put the lid on to prevent evaporation if it seems to be getting too dry.
- ✓ *What's a good taco seasoning recipe?* I use Amy's, right here: http://bit.ly/1bmgY4K Make about 5-10 times the recipe once you know you like it so you always have some on hand.
- ✓ *Will it freeze?* Pasta doesn't do well in the freezer, but this is so easy to throw together with some frozen ingredients, you won't need to freeze leftovers.

Beef and Bean Stew a la Tuscany

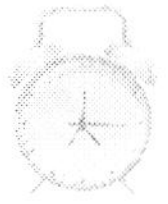
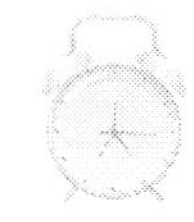
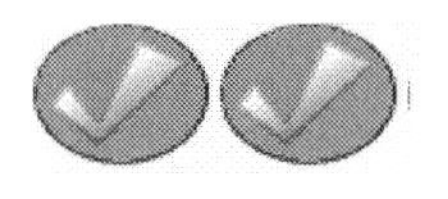

Work Intensity Kid-Friendly Cost

A happy accident as I tried to use up a few ingredients I had lying around, this stew ended up being restaurant-quality and worthy of serving your honored guests.

Ingredients

GF CF If soaking dry beans, start with 1 ¾ cups before soaking.

2 Tbs. each olive oil and butter
4-8 oz. mushrooms, sliced
1 large onion, diced
3-4 cloves garlic, crushed
1-3 lbs. beef for stew or venison roast, cut in 1-2" pieces
2-3 c. beef or bean broth
2 Tbs. tomato paste
15-oz. can diced tomatoes with juice
2 cans white beans, drained and rinsed OR 4 c. cooked dry beans
3-5 carrots, sliced
optional veggies: 2-3 c. spinach or kale, 4-8 oz. fresh or frozen green beans
1/2 tsp. salt
1/2 tsp. pepper
1-2 tsp. Italian seasoning
1-2 Tbs. fresh parsley or 2 tsp. dried
3 sprigs fresh thyme or 1/2 tsp. dried
shredded Parmesan, to serve on top

Method

In a large pot, sauté mushrooms and onions in olive oil and butter until onions are translucent and mushrooms are nicely browned. During the last minute, add crushed garlic to the mix.

Add meat pieces and toss over high heat until browned as well, then put all the other ingredients except the herbs in the pot. Bring to a boil and simmer on very low, covered, for about 2 hours or until the meat is tender and practically falling apart. Ten minutes before serving, add the herbs, fresh or dried. Top with shredded or shaved Parmesan to serve.

Serves 4-8.

Timesaver: Make it in a slow cooker, simply browning beef, onions and mushrooms first and tossing everything in at once. Cook on high for 4 hours or low for 8 hours. Add the herbs during the last 10-30 minutes.

Added Bonus: The stew is perfect for a crowd, since it's easy to double, stretches the meat thus saving money, and can sit on the stovetop to wait until everyone is ready to eat.

Substitutions and Frugal Tips

- ✓ *Substitution ideas:* Make it more elegant by substituting red wine for 1/2 cup of the broth; add it first after sautéing the onions and browning the meat to deglaze, then add the broth and other ingredients.
- ✓ Subtract and insert vegetables to your heart's content.
- ✓ *Serving suggestion:* Try serving over cooked noodles or mashed potatoes.
- ✓ *Make it creamy:* Add 8 oz. of cream cheese or yogurt cheese (http://www.kitchenstewardship.com/WhereWhey) after removing from heat and before serving. Sour cream would be good, too, reminiscent of stroganoff.

FAQs

- ✓ *What do I do with the rest of the can of tomato paste?* Freeze it in 1 Tbs. portions plopped onto waxed paper on a cookie sheet and transfer to a plastic bag for storage.
- ✓ *What is a "white bean"?* You can use great northern, navy, garbanzo or cannellini beans in this recipe.

Mexican Stuffed Peppers

If your family likes Mexican food, this lower carb, grain-free twist on taco night will send you running to buy whole peppers in a hurry!

Ingredients GF CF

½ lb. ground beef
1 Tbs. taco seasoning (or half packet)
1 ½ c. frozen corn (optional)
2 c. black beans or about 1 can, drained and rinsed
1 16 oz. jar salsa
1/4 c. diced red or white onion
(optional) other vegetables: diced red pepper, zucchini, leafy greens, etc… anything you have on hand to enhance the mixture
5 bell peppers, green or colored, halved, seeds removed
shredded cheese, cheddar or Mexican blend

Method

In a medium-sized pot or deep skillet, brown meat and add taco seasoning. Add all the other ingredients except the halved peppers and cheese and heat through on the stovetop over medium heat. Be creative with the vegetables you have on hand; it's hard to go wrong with a whole jar of salsa and some taco seasoning already in the mix!

Meanwhile, use a steamer basket to steam the halved peppers for 5-10 minutes until somewhat softened but not cooked to death (fork tender). Arrange in an oval or 9×13 casserole dish and "stuff" the filling into each pepper generously.

After filling, top the peppers with shredded cheese and broil or bake at 350F for 5-10 minutes to brown the cheese.

Serves 4-6.

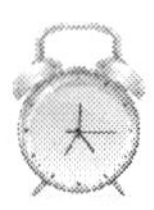

Timesaver: You can skip the steaming peppers step and simply fill the raw peppers and add a little water around them in the casserole dish to soften them up while it bakes. Bake 30 minutes, covered, before removing the cover for 5-10 minutes to brown the cheese.

You can also freeze raw peppers, seeded and cut in half, and then they're ready for the next stuffed pepper meal, especially if you freeze a jar of leftover filling!

Added Bonus: This filling is a bit like the loaves and fishes: everything is suddenly full and there's still more left! I often end up with more filling than I need, which becomes great taco style leftovers or freezes well for later.

Substitutions and Frugal Tips

- ✓ *Substitution ideas:* You might add extra kidney beans or lentils to bulk up for the frugality of only using 1/2 lb. ground beef (about a cup to a cup and a half). Double the taco seasoning to compensate.
- ✓ If you don't need the low carb, grain-free version, add a cup of cooked brown rice into the mix. Be smart and have cooked rice on hand by freezing extras or planning stir fry, Black-Eyed Pea Casserole (p. 85) or Cuban Black Beans Over Rice (p. 67) for the day before.
- ✓ Conversely, the beans could decrease and the meat increase if you're very serious about low carb; I'm more serious about my food budget, so I go the opposite way with meat and beans.
- ✓ It's a perfect recipe to add in some ground beef heart or liver if you're trying to eat more organ meats. For tips, see here: http://www.kitchenstewardship.com/Liver

FAQs

- ✓ *What kind of peppers are best?* Red and green peppers are classic stuffed pepper options, but if you like a little heat, try this recipe with fresh poblanos (amazing!), and if you like a little fanciness, make roasted red peppers and then stuff those.
- ✓ *What do I do with the rest of the meat from a pound?* When browning a half pound ground beef, you might brown a whole pound and freeze the other half (before adding seasoning) for an easy pasta meal the next week. Alternately, brown 2 pounds ground beef, season with the appropriate amount of taco seasoning for that amount, and freeze ¾ of it for tacos another night.

Recipe inspired by Coping with Frugality (http://bit.ly/1hln1D7).

Slow Cooker Lentil Rice Casserole

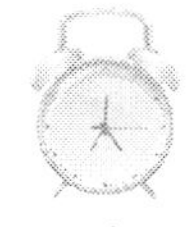
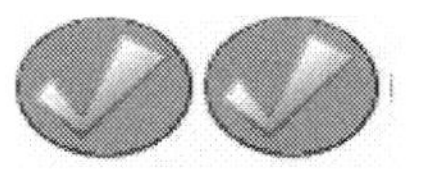

Work Intensity Kid-Friendly Cost

A simple, inexpensive meal that will be ready when you are. Make it Mexican or Italian by changing just a few ingredients and your family won't get tired of it!

Ingredients GF

3/4 c. dry green lentils
1/2 c. brown rice
1 c. water
2 1/2 c. homemade chicken stock
1 c. tomato sauce (8 oz. can) or 1 6-oz. can tomato paste + an extra ½ c. stock
3/4 c. chopped onion OR 3-4 Tbs. dried minced onion
1 c. chopped green or red pepper
1/2-1 c. grated or finely chopped carrot
2 c. cooked, shredded chicken
optional: other vegetables like spinach, broccoli
3 tsp. Italian seasoning or taco seasoning
2 cloves crushed garlic or 1/4-1/2 tsp. garlic powder
1/2 tsp. salt
Dash pepper
1 c. grated cheese (I prefer sharp cheddar, but try a Mexican blend with the taco seasoning or mozzarella with the Italian)
optional: salsa or spaghetti sauce to serve

Method

Combine rice, lentils, and water in the slow cooker following this rice soaking method (http://www.kitchenstewardship.com/FermentedRice). Allow to soak overnight with the cooker turned off. Drain the water, then add all the other ingredients and mix everything together in the slow cooker ***except*** for cheese. Set slow cooker to high for 4 hours or low for 8 hours, adding cheese about a half hour from the end of the time.

Serve with salsa for the Mexican version, and optional heated spaghetti sauce with the Italian.

Serves 4-6.

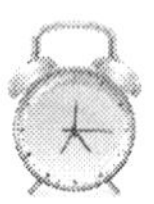

Timesaver: You can prep all the vegetables the night before in a separate container and simply mix in the morning, OR soak the day before and then prep everything in the slow cooker the night before, storing the whole thing in the fridge overnight.

Substitutions and Frugal Tips

- ✓ *Substitution ideas:* You can add just about any vegetable to this dish and it will be excellent. Toss in whatever you need to use up from the fridge!
- ✓ *Need to go meatless?* Just skip the chicken and use vegetable broth instead of chicken stock. It's a very simple dish, but still tasty!

FAQs

- ✓ *What if I don't have a slow cooker?* When I was originally introduced to this dish, the instructions were for a baked casserole. I had a terrible time getting the rice to cook, but no one else in the multitude of comments did, so I must have done something wrong. Check out Getting Freedom From Debt (http://bit.ly/1eO93xq) for the baking instructions.
- ✓ *Freezeable*? No problem. It's so easy, though, I'd recommend just freezing the ingredients, chopped, like peppers and onions, and throwing it all together in the morning for a quick evening meal.

Recipe inspired by Getting Freedom From Debt (http://bit.ly/1eO93xq).

Southwestern Pot Pie

 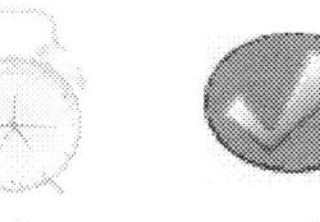 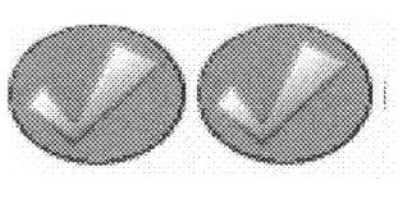   

Work Intensity Kid-Friendly Cost

A hint of autumn sweetness, the heartiness of beans with the sophistication of garbanzos, a little salsa heat…and then cornbread! The flavors in Southwestern Pot Pie seem surprisingly off the wall, but once they're all working together, it's a distinctive dish that will keep you coming back for more.

Ingredients

CF If soaking dry beans, start with ¾-1 cups before soaking.

1 Tbs. oil
1 large onion, chopped (about 1 cup)
2 c. peeled raw sweet potatoes, cut into about 1/2" cubes
1 jar 16 oz. salsa (2 cups)
1/2 c. water
1/4 tsp. ground cinnamon
1 c. frozen corn
1 can (15-16 oz.) garbanzo beans, drained and rinsed, or 2 c. cooked beans
Follow directions to mix up half a batch of cornbread batter (recipe below)

Method

Heat oil in a 4-quart Dutch oven or deep cast iron pot over medium-high heat. Cook onion in oil about 5 minutes, stirring occasionally, until crisp-tender. Stir in sweet potatoes, salsa, water and cinnamon. Heat to boiling; reduce heat. Cover and simmer 20-25 minutes or until sweet potatoes are tender.

While the sweet potato mixture is cooking, preheat your oven to 400F. Mix up a half batch of cornbread batter.

When the sweet potatoes are tender, stir the corn and beans into the pot. If it seems a lot of liquid has evaporated during cooking, you may want to add an extra ¼ cup water at this point. Drop the cornbread batter by large spoonfuls onto vegetable mixture. Bake in the preheated oven, uncovered, for 15-25 minutes until a toothpick inserted (into the dumplings only) comes out clean.

Serves 4-6.

Timesaver: Make a whole batch of cornbread and pour the other half into a loaf pan for dinner the next night. (Chili, anyone? Page 39.)

Added Bonus: Any one-pot meal is an added bonus, right?

Substitutions and Frugal Tips

- ✓ *Substitution ideas:* You can certainly use butternut squash or other orange veggies in place of the sweet potatoes, and if the dish seems too sweet for your tastes, cut back or cut out the cinnamon. Add garlic for a new twist.

- ✓ *Need lower-carb?* Omit the corn or replace it with some chopped peppers or other favorite veggie. Add greens like spinach if you've got them!

FAQs

- ✓ *Can it be gluten-free?* Just use your favorite GF cornbread recipe!

- ✓ *What if I don't have a Dutch oven?* You have three choices. You could bake the cornbread separately and crumble it over the top. You can pour the sweet potato mixture into a 3-quart casserole dish and top with the dumplings, proceeding with the baking instructions as directed. You could also try cooking the dumplings on the stovetop in a covered pot over low heat, but I would just recommend using even less than half the cornbread recipe – keep the dumplings small and spread apart and you should be fine.

Katie's Cornbread (full batch)

Mix together:
1 c. cornmeal (make sure it's not "degerminated")
1 c. whole wheat flour
4 tsp. baking powder
½ tsp. salt
2 Tbs. honey

Make a well and add:
2 beaten eggs
1 c. milk (see below to use yogurt or buttermilk instead)
¼ c. melted coconut oil or butter

Stir until just smooth. Pour into greased 9×9 pan and bake 25 minutes at 400 degrees.

Healthy Upgrade: Soaked

Simply mix the flour and cornmeal with a total of one cup buttermilk or yogurt or a mixture (*instead of* the milk in the original). Set at room temp 12-24 hours and add all the other ingredients at baking time. *Change*: Reduce baking powder to 2 tsp. and add 1 tsp. baking soda.

Hearty Lentil Stew

If it were possible to get zero dollar signs for the cost of the recipe, I'd give it to this one. A very simple meal, it's often our Ash Wednesday and Good Friday fare.

Ingredients GF

2 Tbs. oil
1 chopped onion
2 stalks celery, sliced
2 cloves garlic, minced
1 chopped green pepper
6 c. water or broth
1 c. pearled or hulled barley or brown rice or more lentils
1 c. dry green lentils
1 carrot, shredded
2 c. tomato sauce
2 Tbs. apple cider vinegar
2 Tbs. soy sauce
1 tsp. basil
½ tsp. marjoram
1-1 1/2 tsp. salt, to taste
1/4 tsp. black pepper
optional: shredded cheese

Method

Sauté onion, celery, garlic, and green pepper in a large pot in oil until softened. Add 6 cups water, barley, and lentils. Bring to a boil and reduce heat to low. Stir, cover and cook 30 minutes. Add all the remaining ingredients except cheese, stir, cover and cook 30 minutes. Add optional cheese for the last 5 minutes.

Serve over potatoes or cooked brown rice.

Serves 6-8.

Timesaver: You can also mix it all up and use the slow cooker, on high for 4 hours or low for 6-8. Omit the cheese and add it on top (optionally) for the last half hour.

Added Bonus: With cheese melted on top, it's delicious and delightfully frugal; without cheese, it's positively penitential and even more frugal.

Substitutions and Frugal Tips

- ✓ *Substitution ideas:* Use colored peppers in place of green for a milder taste and toss in greens or other favorite veggies you have on hand.
- ✓ You can also skip the vinegar entirely if you don't like the flavor of vinegar. It does come through in the final product, so for my own tastes, I often cut the amount in half.
- ✓ *Get frugal and nourishing:* Try sprouting your lentils first. Not only do they increase in bulk, saving you money, but the nutrition is pumped up a ton! See instructions here: http://www.kitchenstewardship.com/MMSprout

FAQs

- ✓ *How is this gluten-free?* If you use brown rice in place of the barley and be careful to use GF soy sauce, you've eliminated the gluten.
- ✓ *Can I use quick-cooking barley?* It ends up the same, so yes.
- ✓ *Freezer friendly?* Most definitely.

Healthy Upgrade: Soaked

Just let the barley and lentils soak overnight in warm water. Drain and proceed with the recipe as written, except you'll need to delete a cup of water because the barley and lentils will have soaked up liquid already.

Black-Eyed Pea Casserole

   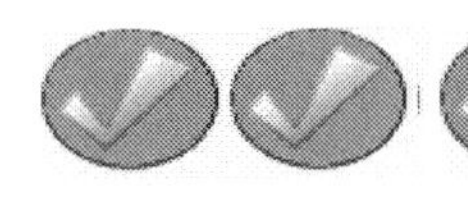   

Work Intensity Kid-Friendly Cost

The simplicity of these ingredients may surprise you when the taste ends up being just right. Comfort food that's totally healthy, in just one pot? That's my kind of meal.

Ingredients GF

If soaking dry beans, start with 1 1/3 cups before soaking.

1 lb. ground beef
1 small onion, diced
½ colored pepper, diced
1 garlic clove, minced
2 (15 oz) cans black-eyed peas, drained OR ~4 c. cooked black-eyed peas
2 c. cooked brown rice
1 (16 oz) can diced tomatoes, undrained
1 c. sharp cheddar cheese
Optional: a few handfuls of spinach, roughly chopped
1/2 tsp. salt
1/4 tsp. pepper

Method

In a large pot, brown meat, onion and pepper and drain well. Add garlic and saute a minute, then mix in all the other ingredients and heat through.

You can also pour into a lightly-greased casserole dish, after mixing but before heating through, and bake uncovered at 350 degrees F for 25 minutes, topped with additional cheese if desired. Serve hot.

Serves 4-8.

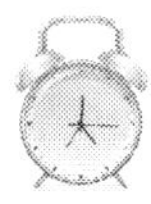

Timesaver: I highly recommend making cooked brown rice on another day, perhaps for stir fry or another rice-based recipe, and simply making a double batch. This meal comes together in no time if that's done and the black-eyed peas are cooked.

Added Bonus: Leftovers can go into a wrap for a totally new meal.

Substitutions and Frugal Tips

- ✓ *Substitution ideas:* This recipe is so simple, it's perfect for adapting to almost any vegetable or meat you have on hand. Try adding bacon or using sausage as the base. Toss in shredded carrots or frozen peas.

- ✓ Many kinds of cheese would work fine.

- ✓ *Not enough flavor for you?* Try taco seasoning, cumin or chili powder to taste, or even Italian seasoning. Start with a teaspoon and allow the dish to cook a while (on the stovetop) to let the flavors meld together, then taste and add more as necessary.

- ✓ *Frugal tip:* Use dry beans and freeze the rest for Black-Eyed Pea Soup, p. 47.

FAQs

- ✓ *What if I don't have cooked brown rice on hand?* To get 2 cups cooked rice, start with 2/3 cups dry brown rice and 1 1/3 cups water. Bring to a boil and cook on your lowest heat setting, covered (no peeking!) for 45 minutes. You can increase digestibility by using this accelerated fermentation rice method (http://www.kitchenstewardship.com/FermentedRice).

- ✓ *Freezer friendly?* Not a problem. This is a good candidate for a double batch once you know your family likes it. Just spread the thawed mixture in a casserole dish and follow the baking instructions with extra cheese on top.

Adapted from Girls to Grow (http://bit.ly/1eO9yYo)

Grain-Free Fudgy Brownies

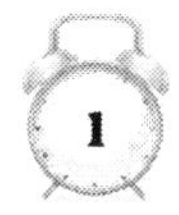
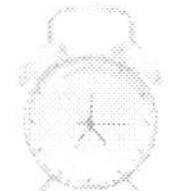
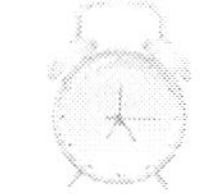

Work Intensity Kid-Friendly Cost

I know, a brownie recipe in a bean book. You'll have to trust me on this one. No one will ever, ever guess what your secret ingredient is, and they'll all be blown away that there's not one speck of flour in the whole thing.

Ingredients GF CF

If soaking dry beans, start with one scant cup before soaking.

1 ¾ c. cooked black beans, or one can, drained and rinsed well
3 eggs (or 2 large eggs)
1/4 c. melted butter or coconut oil, either refined or unrefined
¼ c. cocoa powder
a pinch of salt (if using home-cooked beans, none for canned beans)
1 tsp. vanilla
½ c. honey OR 3/4 c. sugar or sucanat
½ c. chocolate chips (optional, but helpful)
1/3 c. walnuts (optional)

Method

Grease an 8x8 glass baking dish. In a food processor, blend everything but the chocolate chips and walnuts until absolutely, totally smooth. Fold in the chocolate chips and nuts (or you can sprinkle these on top in the pan). Pour into the greased pan and bake in a preheated 350F oven for 30-40 minutes. The brownies are done when a toothpick or knife inserted comes out clean, more or less. Watch the edges for blackening/drying out if you're unsure. Store at room temperature for a few days, but any longer than that demands cold storage for these goodies.

Makes 16 squares.

Timesaver: Cook up a big batch of black beans for Black Bean Soup (p. 51), Cuban Beans and Rice (p. 66) or Veggie Bean Burritos (p. 25) and make these for dessert.

Added Bonus: Seriously. A dessert that is nearly health food, but still tastes like a dessert? Serve it with some ice cream and a pat on the back for a job well done. ;)

Substitutions and Frugal Tips

- ✓ *Brownie flavor variations:*

  - ✓ **Coconut brownies**: Use unrefined, virgin coconut oil and dust the top of the brownies with shredded coconut (mostly just to alert your eaters that they're choosing a mildly coconut flavored brownie).

  - ✓ **Minty brownies**: Add a few drops of peppermint extract or peppermint oil (like that used for rock candy). Or simply make the brownies after making this Peppermint Pattie bark (http://bit.ly/1bJsuBM) and don't rinse the food processor.

- ✓ *Can I toss in extra beans?* Unlike most of my favorite bean recipes, do not "toss in extras" to this recipe. Be sure to measure the cooked beans carefully even if you're soaking beans just for this recipe.

  In fact, there's an appreciable consistency difference between the final product using a can of beans vs. home-cooked beans. I recommend the can for your first try, unless you absolutely feel the need to soak.

- ✓ Also, I don't recommend previously frozen home-cooked beans. You can get very good results with home-cooked beans, but the brownies get a little chalky if the beans have been frozen.

Recipe adapted from Natural Fertility and Wellness (http://bit.ly/Or2xly).

Other Bean Recipes and Resources

I hosted a huge carnival with over 60 recipes from many of my favorite bloggers (and some lesser-known treasures, too). Find it here: http://www.kitchenstewardship.com/BeansCarnival

More bean recipes I've tried or have bookmarked:

- Crispy Roasted Chickpeas (http://bit.ly/1aRRATK)
- Black Bean, Squash and Swiss Chard Chili (http://bit.ly/NzefdF)
- 9 Incredible Bean Recipes from a KS Reader (http://www.kitchenstewardship.com/MalloryBeans)
- Baked Beans with a Kick (http://bit.ly/1bSyNGg)
- Homemade Baked Bean Recipe (http://bit.ly/1lwK8Pb)
- White Bean Vanilla Cake (http://bit.ly/LSnV18)
- Resource: How to Can Dry Beans Quickly (http://bit.ly/1gmmaEy)
- Resource: How to Pressure Can Dry Beans (http://bit.ly/1dFtxT5)

Note: These links were all active at the time of publishing, but I cannot guarantee that all the recipes will remain available online.

Index: Recipes by the Bean

Index: Recipes by Dietary Restrictions

Meatless

Gluten Free

Find Your Food Index

If you've got something you need to use up, this is the place to look. Recipes listed include those that call for the food and those that could include it if you'd like. So many recipes in this book use carrots, peppers, celery and onions that I didn't bother to include them on this list. Just point and shoot if you've got something like that you need to get rid of!

Acknowledgements:
Books are never written solo, at least not well, and no recipe should be loved by only one family before becoming famous. I relied on a huge team of people to make this book what it is, including readers who commented on the original posts where a few of these recipes were shared.

Thank you to so many:

My depth of gratitude belongs to my fearless editor, Lenetta Kuehn of Nettacow (http://bit.ly/1iLYXfL), who keeps me in check and makes sure I can spell correctly, too. I also had some backup editors in Pam of Brown Thumb Mama (http://bit.ly/1bJvf61) and Frances Liberto, two more reasons why this book rocks.

For the first time, I invited readers to become recipe testers for eBooks, and over 200 stepped up to the challenge. To the two dozen of you who ran these recipes through the wringer, I'm so pleased you helped out, and you'll see many of your edits and questions answered in this final text. Thank you for increasing the quality of my work so very much!

And of course, the biggest honor goes to my personal beans testers and the ones who have to put up with me typing recipe updates during dinner while they tell me which of two similar dishes they like best: my dear family, especially my husband, who puts up with an awful lot from me.

Please visit KitchenStewardship.com for more nutritious recipes, kitchen tips and a healthy dose of wit, or if you'd like to check out other digital and print cookbooks, also found on Amazon.